Overcoming Food Allergies

Also Available!

Overcoming Food

Allergies

Your Roadmap to Effective Diagnosis and Health Strategies

Dr Arif Ahmed

with Dr Sowmya Nagarajan

Hay House Publishers India

New Delhi • London • Sydney

Carlsbad, California • New York City

Hay House Publishers (India) Pvt. Ltd.
Muskaan Complex, Plot No.3, B-2 Vasant Kunj, New Delhi-110 070, India
Hay House Inc., PO Box 5100, Carlsbad, CA 92018-5100, USA
Hay House UK, Ltd., The Sixth Floor, Watson House, 54 Baker Street, W1U 7BU, UK
Hay House Australia Pty Ltd., 18/36 Ralph St., Alexandria NSW 2015, Australia

Email: contact@hayhouse.co.in
www.hayhouse.co.in

ISBN 978-81-19554-04-1
ISBN 978-81-19554-05-8 (ebook)

Printed at Repro India Limited

Dedication

To my parents, who emphasised the importance of healthy natural food and a holistic lifestyle.

Contents

Section IV
Management

Section V
Specific Food Triggers and Additives

Section VI
Miscellaneous

Appendix I

Appendix II

Appendix III

Preface

All of of us eat to live and most of us enjoy eating different foods. However, research has shown that worldwide about 1 in 20 children or adults have an allergy to at least one food, which is an increasing problem since the beginning of this century. This is also happening in India. Therefore, as food allergy has now become a major health issue, it is of utmost importance to educate society on food allergy.

When a person has a food allergy, it will affect the whole family, especially when a child is involved. This will cause daily anxiety (mainly in the parents) about the risk of accidental exposure to the food which could lead to severe and dangerous symptoms, such as anaphylaxis.

This book is a unique book, based on a highly scientific background, giving important information on the various aspects of food allergies and related adverse reactions to food additives, in both adults and children. The book is put together by various co-authors who are very experienced in the complex topic of food allergy, covering the topic of food allergy in an understandable way for both doctors and readers with no medical training.

It is crucial that the awareness of food allergies in India receives more attention. Many still believe that food allergy is uncommon and that its prevalence is low. However, the world has now been witnessing a real food allergy epidemic, which makes it important to create awareness regarding this health issue in India.

This book aims to educate patients and families with food allergies, clinicians, nutritionists, and other allied professionals interested in adverse food reactions. Moreover, the book offers an important source of information that can be used in creating awareness in schools and workplaces. The book is also a practical guide, with coverage of unique aspects of food allergy in each chapter. Taken together, all chapters will give the reader comprehensive and practical information on food allergy and the ongoing research and developments relating to food allergy.

I strongly recommend the book to all who are interested in food allergies.

—Prof. Hugo Van Bever
Professor, Department of Paediatrics,
Yong Loo Lin School of Medicine, National University of Singapore

Foreword

Overcoming Food Allergies features the aetiology and impact that food allergy has on patients and delves into some of the challenges associated with diagnoses and treatment options and their limitations. The book underscores the unmet needs in this area and brings to the fore evidence-based information on prompt recognition of food allergy reactions and potentially significant impact and management approaches to improve health and quality of life of those with food allergies. More importantly, it highlights the significance of lifestyle practices and traditional approaches that make our immune system capable of dealing with various antigens including food allergens, which unfortunately are waning.

The prevalence of food allergies is increasing in India, and the knowledge and practices around the subject are poor. That way, this book is timely and will serve as a tool for all the stakeholders and the public to effectively prevent and manage food allergies.

—Dr Hemalatha R.

MBBS MD, FNAMS, FIUNS, FTAS
Director, ICMR-National Institute of Nutrition, DHR, MoHFW, GOI
President, Nutrition Society of India
EC Member, Federation of Asian Nutrition Societies (FANS)
Chairperson, National Committee for International Union of Nutrition Sciences (IUNS)

Why I Wrote the Book

'The way you think, the way you behave, the way you eat, can influence your life by 30 to 50 years.'
—Deepak Chopra

After the great reception of my earlier book, *Winning Over Allergies: Myths and Facts*, I was encouraged by friends and patients to write a book on food allergy. I felt that the above book was sufficient enough until I had the opportunity to visit and spend a considerable amount of time in a remote village located in the eastern part of India.

Everyone in this village would either walk or use a bicycle to commute around for work and pleasure. There were no TV sets and no mobile phones. The children all played out in the open areas and would regularly attend the local school. The people living in the village looked fit and healthy and there seemed to be no cases of diabetes, hypertension, or allergies.

I soon realised that although the people of this village had no connection to urban life and weren't well off economically, their diet was far superior to us city folks living in urban areas with the best of malls and food outlets. They ate everything that was fresh and natural. Their vegetables, fruits, grains, and meat were far superior in quality and taste compared to the ones we consumed in the city. It was free of all preservatives and colourants. Also, the children ate no junk foods and were breastfed in infancy which was followed by homemade complimentary feeds. It brought back memories of my childhood days in my rural hometown.

This motivated me to write a book not only to make people aware of the widely prevalent food allergies but also to make them aware that how far we have come from our natural habitat into a world of modernity and thus paying a price in the form of lifestyle disorders like allergies notwithstanding other rampant non-communicable diseases.

How to Use the Book

Whether you have picked up this book because you are personally suffering or have a near and dear one suffering from a food allergy, you belong to the medical field and thus the interest, or you have a general interest in the field and like to further your knowledge, I suggest reading the book cover to cover as it covers the topic of food allergy in a comprehensive yet concise manner.

The chapters are arranged in a format that firstly provides a basic introduction to different food allergies which is then followed by the chapters that explore their impact on health and ways to deal with food allergy and food intolerance. Also, to make the information more practical and easier to correlate, important individual foods are given in detail followed by real-life case scenarios. You will also find some medical terms throughout the book and if you want to understand these terms in detail, please refer to the Glossary section. Apart from it, if you need additional sources for further reading, you can refer to the References section at the end of the book.

All in all, the aim of the book is not just to educate you about food allergies but also to help you deal holistically with the problem.

Section I
INTRODUCTION

1
Allergy Overview

'If music is the food of love, play on.'

From *Twelfth Night* by William Shakespeare

Food essentially is the basic love of all humans across regions and cultures. However, humankind, like Orsino in the famous play, has indulged and abused food in different ways. Among the resultant effects, food allergies are extremely concerning because of their severe consequences including death. But before we start with the topic of food allergies, let's see the changes when it comes to the food we eat and how we consume it.

We started off as hunter-gatherers and for millions of years, we ate only natural, uncooked, or partially cooked food. Hence, our entire digestive system evolved to this particular style of food and cooking style. But our eating habits and patterns have drastically changed over the last few centuries, leading to innumerable disorders. This is best described as lifestyle disorder due to a geno-environmental interaction and a very prevalent but less commonly known disorders consist of food allergies and food intolerance.

We will go through these different food disorders to bring about much-needed awareness regarding this subject. Pharmacotherapy or drugs forms a minuscule section in the treatment and prevention of food disorders while the preventive measures encompass a vast section of this field including nutrition and breastfeeding. We cannot go back in time to become hunter-gatherers again but we can definitely make our food as natural as possible with the best of the available techniques.

2

The Burden of Food Allergy

This chapter outlines the burden of food allergy, its worldwide prevalence, and its comparison across the world. The chapter also addresses how food allergies affect the quality of life and what is not a food allergy.

Introduction

Food Allergy (FA) has become a prevalent public health issue, both worldwide and in India. But the term 'food allergy' is mostly incorrectly used by patients and healthcare professionals alike. Many people casually describe themselves as a little allergic to very common food substances and do not fully understand what is implied by the term 'allergic'. A major reason for this is that any adverse reaction to food often gets wrongly labelled as a food allergy. Another cause of this misunderstanding in the community is incorrect and irresponsible coverage of the topic by the media. Also, some alternative medicine therapists misdiagnose a health issue as an allergy, which also contributes to the problem.

In this chapter, we will explore the terminologies related to food allergies in a simple manner.

Definition of Food Allergy

Food allergy is best explained as an immune system response to a food item/ingredient where the body mistakenly believes that that particular food is harmful to itself. When a person with a food allergy consumes food to which they are allergic, their immune system releases increased amounts of chemicals, including histamine, which starts a cascade of reactions, affecting the respiratory system, the gastrointestinal tract, the skin, and/or the cardiovascular system. Therefore, correct and early recognition is extremely important in such cases as it allows to the provision of timely and proper healthcare.

The Burden of the Disease

It is estimated that food allergy affects around 7-8 per cent of children in the United States and under 2 per cent of children in India. Though this might not be a high number, it does undermine the difficulties faced by people suffering from food allergies and their families as well. This can include regular office visits or emergency department visits, arranging rescue medications, hospitalisations, and non-medical expenses such as lost productivity and impaired quality of life. Not much data is available in India about the economic burden of food allergies, though some data is available from the United States and Europe.

Centre for Disease Control and Prevention (CDC) states that food allergy prevalence has seen a 50 per cent increase in the early 2000s (1997-2011) in children.

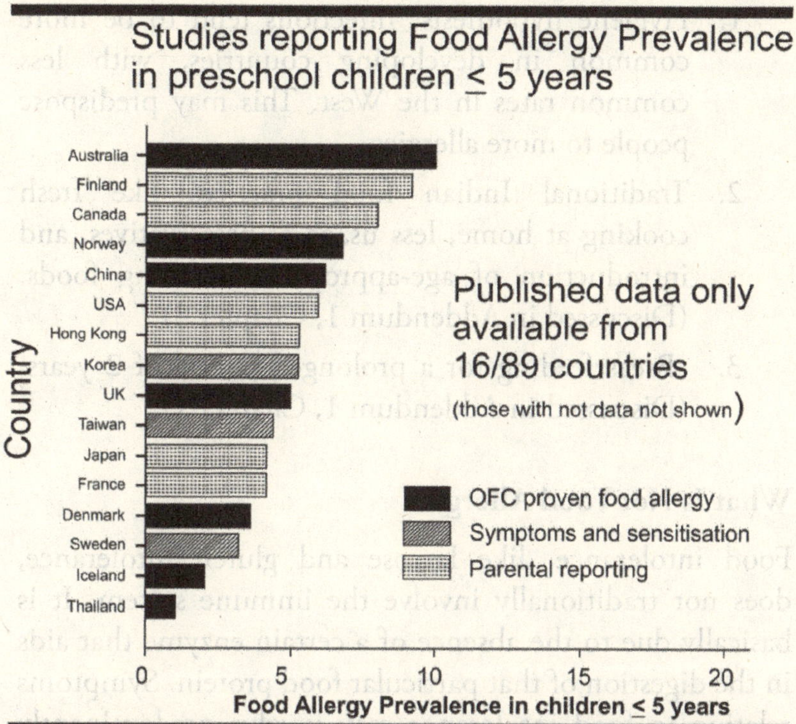

Prescott et al. World Allergy Organisation Journal 2013, 6:21

Common Foods Causing Food Allergy

The top eight food allergens that cause food allergy include milk, egg, wheat, peanut, tree nuts, soy, fish, and shellfish and they contribute to almost 90 per cent of FA reactions, even though there are reported over 150 possible foods which can cause food allergy. This trend seems more prevalent in the West as compared to South and East Asia including India. Children of Indian descent, reared in the West, are reported to have more food allergies than Indian kids raised in India. There are many reasons for it, a few being:

1. Hygiene hypothesis: Infections tend to be more common in developing countries, with less common rates in the West. This may predispose people to more allergies.
2. Traditional Indian food practices like fresh cooking at home, less usage of preservatives, and introduction of age-appropriate weaning foods. (Discussed in Addendum 1, Chapter 3)
3. Breastfeeding for a prolonged period of 2 years. (Discussed in Addendum 1, Chapter 1)

What Is Not Food Allergy?

Food intolerance, like lactose and gluten intolerance, does not traditionally involve the immune system. It is basically due to the absence of a certain enzyme that aids in the digestion of that particular food protein. Symptoms relating to food intolerance may involve predominantly the gastrointestinal system issues like diarrhoea, bloating sensation, and abdominal cramps among others. The other systems of the body are simply not involved.

Importance of Food Allergy Field

In the medical world, allergy is not given due importance, with a deficiency of formal allergy training programs, especially in India. There is no undergraduate teaching in allergy and in postgraduate teaching, allergy training is limited to a few diseases. Hence, this leads to a deficiency in medical care rendered in this field. Much of the information we have about food allergy is derived from the West and may not extrapolate to the Indian population.

Thus, it is important to recognise the importance of FA as it is an evolving problem and ignorance of the same can be fatal. A child of Indian parents, living in Australia and sensitised to peanuts and some tree nuts, accidentally got exposed to these foods in a Thai restaurant where he developed an anaphylactic reaction rapidly. Unfortunately, he did not have an epinephrine (a lifesaving drug) auto-injector on hand and was rushed to the hospital immediately where he received an epinephrine injection. Therefore, we can see that awareness of these problems usually goes a long way in helping FA patients.

The new reports project the possibility of increasing incidences and prevalence of FA in the Asian and African sub-continent as these economies expand and their lifestyle become more westernised. This also leads to increased levels of air pollution, which may cause oxidative stress, which indirectly predisposes people to atopic diseases. Until such a time, when a therapeutic tool is available to treat FA, we should continue to educate our medical graduates about allergic diseases and manage FA conservatively. The trend of food allergy also calls for more streamlining of training programs for allergy/immunology, in the background of the latest guidelines of early introduction of allergenic foods and more use of oral food challenges in the diagnosis of food allergy.

If the increased tendency to adopt the Western lifestyle continues, and we don't address this issue at its present through awareness programs, education, and research, there is no reason to believe that this problem will fade away and the number of people suffering because of food allergy will continue to rise.

Case Scenario

See the case scenario section in Section VI, Chapter 2, 'The Impact of Food Allergies' for more details.

Salient Points

- Lack of formal allergy training among medical professionals in India and decreased awareness of allergies in the general public is a leading cause for mismanagement of allergies.
- Increasing awareness and educating the masses about allergic diseases can help improve quality of life.

3

Hygiene Hypothesis

The hygiene hypothesis gives a plausible explanation for the increasing incidence of allergies throughout the world.

Introduction

The hygiene hypothesis was first introduced by Strachan in 1989. He first noticed an association between smaller families and an increased risk of allergies. An observational study done in the UK, in the early 1950s, suggested an inverse relationship between allergic diseases and the number of older siblings.

An important aspect of the immune system is for the cells to recognise and neutralise pathogens and sometimes one's own dead cells. Healthy cells in the body have a distinctive mechanism to recognise one's own cells, while foreign cells are marked out for careful screening. If these foreign cells cause too much harm, the immune cells attack them and take note of them so that they can act against them faster, if any repeat encounters do occur in the future.

Environmental Exposure

Mainly, microorganisms are known to help in the development of antibodies in the immune system and thereby have a proactive role against the development of allergies. But in early 20th century, the infections became more rampant, and this was followed by better sanitation and catch-up vaccinations due to industrialisation and urbanisation.

Over the last decade or so, infectious diseases have decreased and thereby exposure to some microorganisms, which may have boosted the immune system. This is believed to have resulted in the compromised function of the immune system and an increase in the prevalence of allergies.

If the immune system does not properly identify a foreign substance, it may overreact to harmless substances, causing allergic reactions, like anaphylaxis to bee-sting or fire ants or foods. In the Western world, the percentage of children who suffer from immune system hyper-responsiveness (allergies and asthma) has roughly doubled in the past 50 years, even as infectious diseases have become much less common, mainly due to improved hygiene, water, sewage treatment, and so on. The increased prevalence of allergies and asthma is likely due in part to the fact that the environments we live in are getting cleaner (because of sanitisers also, now!) and missing opportunities for our immune system to get exposed to many pathogens. In India too, we are seeing an increase in allergic disorders, as we are moving away from traditional lifestyles and eating habits and incorporating Western lifestyles.

The human gut too has many microbiotas which have a protective effect. The widespread and abusive use of antibiotics especially in the first year of life destroys this friendly bacterium which otherwise would have protected against allergies. In addition, the frequent use of H2 blockers as anti-reflux medication affects the pH or lowers the acidity of the stomach. This acid milieu would otherwise have destroyed the allergic substances.

Just as children retain good memory of different languages when trained younger, similarly our immune system retains good memory to differentiate harmless foreign substances from real pathogens, when exposed early in life.

Another factor is that exposure to animal faeces is more common in developing countries where domestic animals and their animal faeces may not be properly contained or separated from domestic environments. In South and East Asia, especially in the Indian sub-continent, cow dung has been regularly used to clean the household areas like the front of the house and the living quarters, in rural areas. In this way, humans are exposed more to the microbiota. It is worthwhile thinking about the possible correlation of decreased atopic diseases in the rural community as seen in children who are raised on farms and have more siblings. However, there are some practices using cow dung that may have been beneficial at a point in time but would be detrimental now; one of these is using it as a fuel for cooking. It only increases indoor pollution and adds to global warming.

Case Scenario

My parents belonged to the upper-middle-income group. My mother had 9 siblings while I have 4 siblings. However, I have only two children. This is a standard pattern across the same socio-economic group on a secular basis across the Indian subcontinent. Western society was able to reach this stage in the sixties while we in India are achieving this level at the beginning of the twenty-first century. With this small family size and increasing hygiene, we can expect an epidemic of allergic diseases in the Indian diaspora as currently seen in the Western world.

Salient Points

- Exposure to microbes early in life may help develop protection from allergies.
- Adoption of the Western lifestyle, sanitisation, immunisation, and increased personal hygiene has been associated with the prevalence of increasing allergic disorders.

Section II

CLINICAL ASPECTS OF FOOD ALLERGY

1

The Body's Defence Mechanism

In this chapter, details pertaining to the body defence system have been presented in a simplified manner so as to make it easier for the audience to understand, especially given the scenario of Covid 19. The chapter also explores the importance of a robust immune system in fighting infections.

Introduction

The immune system is the body's defence system. It is basically like our army, guarding us against foreign infiltration of viruses, bacteria, and other pathogens. It is also due to the immune system that pathological reactions to harmless substances occur which is also termed as an allergic reaction.

The immune system is divided into two categories: innate and adaptive immune systems. Innate and adaptive immune systems both play a role in allergy. Allergic reactions are the result of sensitisation to harmless substances in the environment, food, or drugs. Upon subsequent re-exposure to these particles, reactions ensue.

The innate immune system is non-specific in nature and acts against all foreign substances entering the body. This involves:

1. Epithelial barriers such as skin and mucous membranes which line the body cavity like the mouth, nose, and intestines.
2. Bony structures like the skull and ribs, which act as shields for internal organ systems from exposure to microorganisms.
3. Inflammatory responses which include proteins produced by body cells and can mount a response to invading pathogens.

The adaptive immune system is very specific as compared to the innate immune system. It is involved in response to bacterial and viral components and produces antibodies specific to the antigen/target encountered. These protective antibodies circulate in the bloodstream to interact with that specific antigen or allergen.

This immune system protects our body against bacteria, pathogens, and foreign particles, resulting in a specific controlled response with the pathogen being cleared from the body and the resolution of the inflammatory processes which are involved in the immune reaction. In susceptible individuals, sometimes, the innate immune system can respond abnormally to inoculated environmental substances, resulting in an allergic reaction.

Role of the Immune System in Allergy (Innate Immune System)

The innate immune systems are associated with the initial response of our body akin to the border security forces. Upon exposure to the microbes/inoculated particles, it mediates the development of the sensitisation process, which later leads to an allergic reaction upon exposure to the same offending allergen. The response is mainly due to the fact that many of these molecules are not found in our body and are very unique as compared to certain pathogens like coronavirus.

The innate immune system is present since birth and does not adapt as the person grows, unlike the adaptive immune system which can develop memory throughout life. Examples of innate immunity include skin and mucosal barriers which act as physical anatomical barriers along with protective mechanisms such as coughing, sneezing, and vomiting.

Many cell lines in the blood are also involved in the function of the innate immune system. They include:

- Phagocytic cells which include neutrophils, eosinophils, and macrophages. These cells are drawn to pathogens in the body by the process of inflammation and remove them by ingesting them.
- Inflammatory mediators which include basophils and mast cells. They signal the body to mount an inflammatory response if a foreign particle invades.
- Natural killer cells: In the innate immune system, these cells recognise cells under stress or invasion from pathogens and bind to them.
- Molecules including complement proteins and cytokines may stimulate inflammatory processes.

All of the above constitute the initial response which in the country's defence would be done by the border patrol.

Hyper-responsiveness of the Innate Immune System and Allergy

On a few occasions, an exaggerated immune response is mounted against a harmless substance. This is ignored by the innate immune system in the majority of people, but in some, it causes an exaggerated response which can lead to tissue damage in the person's body and in rare cases, even death. When these exaggerated immune responses involve allergens such as dust and pollen, they are termed allergic reactions or type 1 hypersensitivity reaction.

Sensitisation

Sensitisation refers to the development of abnormal adaptive immune response and allergy. It is an important step in an allergic reaction as discussed earlier. This response to an innocent antigen/substance, usually harmless to the majority of people, is mainly a part of the adaptive immune system.

This occurs when an innocent specific trigger leads to the development of antibodies from the adaptive immune system, which in itself may not be responsible for causing an immune reaction. Sensitisation does happen when the person is exposed to the particle in question for the first time followed by the production specific antibodies to the allergen. If the body mistakes a harmless particle for a harmful substance the initial response by the innate immune system causes the production of IgE antibodies by the acquired immune system. To cite an example, specific antibodies are produced against the pollen of parthenium, when the predisposed person is exposed to parthenium pollen for the first time.

These allergen-specific IgE antibodies then inhibit the mast cells by binding the IgE-specific receptors on these mast cells. These mast cells are partly responsible for being the link between the innate and the acquired immune. They are also responsible for perpetuating a potential increase in allergic reactions upon subsequent exposure to the specific antigen.

Classically, an allergic reaction occurs as early as 15-20 minutes of exposure to a specific allergen. It is further divided into early and latephase responses.

- **Early-phase response**

The early phase response is mediated by IgE antibodies. It usually occurs within 2 to 4 hours of exposure. When the same antigen enters the body on subsequent exposure, it interacts with the same specific IgE antibodies on mast cells. This leads to mast cell degranulation or breakdown and the release of inflammatory mediators, causing an allergic reaction.

- **Late-phase response**

The late phase response occurs several hours later, usually starting 4 hours after contact with the allergen. It can last 12 to 24 hours in some individuals. This response occurs in response to inflammation, which catalyses the recruitment of phagocytic cells. These cells release inflammatory mediators, including mast cells that lead to continued allergic symptoms.

- **Secondary immune response**

IgE production by B cells during the late phase of allergic reactions causes a secondary immune response. Exposure to an allergen and the associated inflammatory response have a threshold-lowering effect concerning future exposure; meaning that affected individuals become more sensitive to the allergen with increasing exposure. The inflammatory mediators produced can have a cascading effect on various organ systems including skin, cardiovascular, respiratory, and gastrointestinal symptoms among others. The secondary immune response is akin to the response of the standing or the recruited soldiers.

Atopy

The tendency to develop allergic reactions has a strong hereditary factor which is termed atopy. Approximately 30-40 per cent of the population is atopic, and two-thirds of this subset has allergic diseases. It is still unknown why some people have this abnormal reaction to harmless substances in the environment, or why certain substances are more likely to cause allergies than others.

Salient Points

- The immune system is the body's defence system which fights foreign pathogens.
- The immune system causes a reaction to harmless substances in the majority of the population and this is termed as allergies.
- People most at risk for allergies are those with genetic predisposition and such individuals are labelled as atopic.

2

Terminologies

This chapter briefly classifies the different food terminologies including food idiosyncrasy, food allergy, and food intolerance along with their subtypes. It also familiarises readers with frequently used terminologies with context to food allergies.

Food Allergy

Food Allergy is defined as an adverse health effect arising from a specific immune response that occurs reproducibly on exposure to a given food. This implies that whenever the person is exposed to the same food in the same amount, there shall be a repeated similar effect because of the involvement of their immune system. Non-allergic adverse reactions to foods may be the result of food intolerances or adverse physiologic reactions.

Food allergy is usually IgE mediated and is also known as a hypersensitivity reaction. This generally occurs in young children and is the most frequently seen and the most well-characterised food allergic disorder. However, several non-IgE mediated immunological reactions have been delineated as well.

Specifically, the term food allergy is used when a causal relationship (ideally, with a specific immunological mechanism) has been defined. There are three broad groups of immune reactions: IgE mediated, non-IgE mediated, and mixed. The IgE mediated reactions are usually divided into immediate-onset reactions (arising up to 2 hours from the food ingestion) and immediate plus late-phase (in which the immediate onset symptoms are followed by prolonged or ongoing symptoms). Non-IgE mediated reactions, which are poorly defined both clinically and scientifically, are believed to be generally T-cell mediated. They are typically delayed in onset and occur 4 to 28 hours after ingestion of the offending food(s). Mixed-IgE and non-IgE mediated reactions are conditions associated with food allergy involving both IgE and non-IgE mediated mechanisms.

Adverse Reactions to Food

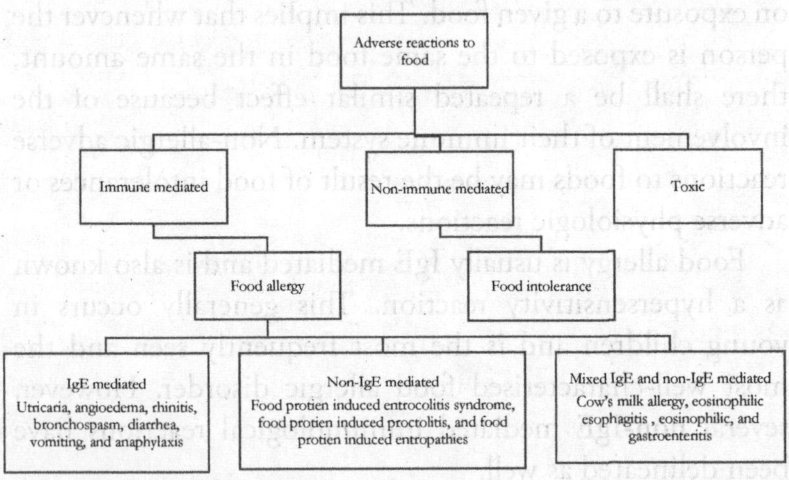

Food Intolerances

These are the most common adverse food reactions which occur due to an inherent factor in the ingested food such as toxin contaminants, pharmaceutical properties of food, and host characteristics such as enzyme deficiency or an idiosyncratic response.

Food Aversion

Food aversion or psychological food intolerance are akin to adverse food reactions, but they cannot be reproduced when the patient is given the food in a blinded fashion or without his knowledge.

Case Scenario

A 35-year-old man walked into my chamber accompanied by his wife. He was adamant that he had a tomato allergy because the moment he would eat a tomato in any form, he would get generalised itching but without any rash. Sometimes there would be retching but rarely there was vomiting.

His wife confided in confidence that sometimes she would slip in tomato in the curries and he wouldn't get any symptoms until informed about it. I did a prick-to-prick test with a fresh tomato in my clinic. There was no reaction. A blood test too showed no increase in value. This is an example of psychological food intolerance which is prevalent in the community.

Salient Points

- Each terminology has a different underlying disease leading to a different outcome.

3

IgE Mediated Food Allergy

This chapter expands on IgE mediated food allergy or the true food allergy in detail.

Introduction

The food allergies which are most concerning and severely affect the quality of life are the IgE mediated food allergies. This is principally because these allergies can cause a life-threatening reaction called anaphylaxis (see Chapter 6 for more details).

Prevalence

The precise prevalence of food allergy is unknown, but surveys have shown that the prevalence of food allergy based on public perception runs as high as 20 per cent, whereas the true prevalence is around 2-8 per cent. The prevalence of food allergy is more common in early childhood days (6-8 per cent) as compared to in adulthood (1-2 per cent).

The prevalence of food allergies in children living in India is unknown but presumed to be lower than in children of Indian descent who are born and brought up in the West. In general, 6–8 per cent of children who are born and brought up in the West are known to have food allergies. This vast difference in prevalence occurs as allergy depends upon epigenetics which is the change of expression of a certain gene in response to environmental changes despite having the same genetic code.

Role of the Environment

The environment plays a crucial role when it comes to allergies. The Westernised standards of living consist of a very hygienically maintained environment, food habits that comprise packed and processed foods that contain additives, preservatives and/or colouring agents, different in dietary choices, and lack of adequate breastfeeding during infancy along with the use of non-traditional food during the weaning phase. All these factors contribute to a high allergy rate in such regions.

As for Indians living in India, due to their cultural and food habits, they are protected from developing these allergies. However, if there is a change in these habits and an adoption of the Western ways in day-to-day living, food allergies will soon become endemic in India as well.

Diagnosis

The whole process of diagnosing a food allergy is somewhat akin to a criminal investigation for repeated thefts occurring in a town. It's quite possible that the patients would attribute their allergy to a particular food item, when in reality, that particular food item may have been like the innocent bystander at the probable scene of the crime.

The normal practice of the police is to arrest all the suspects and keep them behind bars, hoping that this would bring the crime rate down. This unfortunately has become the standard approach in regular clinical practice as well. Physicians impose severe restrictions on the diet of the affected patient and this leads not only to severe nutritional deprivation but also has a psychological impact on the quality of life in these patients.

Although the main suspects with a criminal record would be more likely the incriminating cause, it's plausible that an unexpected person could also have been the cause. The common incriminating foods have been mentioned below. Just as the criminal would undergo a lie detector test, the patient would be asked to undergo a challenge test with the suspected food items, when the clinician is not sure of the incriminating food that is causing the allergy.

Common Foods That Cause Food Allergy

The common food items that cause food allergies differ based on the age bracket. The details have been given below:

1. Infants: Milk and egg
2. Toddlers and Children: Egg, milk, soy, wheat, and peanuts
3. Adolescents and Adults: Peanut, tree nuts, fish, and shellfish

Note: Rice, chickpea, sesame, and lentils are reported to cause food allergy in Indians, though more studies are required.

What Is the Basic Information Required to Manage a Food Allergy?

1. **Food presumed to have provoked the allergic reaction without convincing history**

   It so happens that the patient would attribute the reaction to a particular food. For example, if the patient informs that the reaction is being caused by prawns, then it is necessary to enquire in detail about the preparation of the prawns since any ingredients added in the preparation of the prawns can be the real cause. And it is possible that on previous occasions, the same spice or vegetable may have gone into the preparation of the prawns. Only a clinical reaction within 4 hours of consumption of a raw, boiled prawn can be considered as a true prawn allergy. Also, this test needs to be done on an empty stomach. Another point to note here is that any reaction cannot be considered a food allergy, if symptoms occur several days after eating the prawn. Hence, a detailed history needs to be taken of not only the incriminating food but of every ingredient which may have been used in its preparation.

2. **Quantity of the suspected food consumed**

   A food substance in a small quantity may sometimes not be sufficient enough to cause an allergic reaction. At other times, a food ingredient in combination with another food ingredient could lead to a reaction rather than by itself. In some children, there may be an adverse reaction even to the touch of milk or to the fumes of a frying fish. (See Section 6, Chapter2)

3. **The time gap between consumption and symptom development**

   The time gap is an essential component for narrowing the reaction-causing substance. An IgE mediated allergic food reaction would usually occur from something as short as a few minutes to a maximum of two hours. It would be a rare event for a reaction to occur after two hours and it never occurs beyond the six hours mark.

4. **A history of similar food consumption on other occasions**

   A food causing an allergic reaction would cause a similar reaction every time that it was consumed. If the same food does not cause a reaction under similar circumstances, then it is quite unlikely to be the incriminating agent.

5. **Involvement of other factors such as exercise, alcohol intake, concurrent medications, and menses**

   There are certain foods such as wheat, which under normal circumstances would not cause any reaction. However, if the same food was eaten and the patient would indulge in certain activities such as exercising along with a bath, then there could be a reaction. (See Chapter 7)

6. **Time gap since the last reaction**

   There is no specified time gap required between two episodes of an allergic reaction. However, if there is a history of severe allergic reactions to any food, like anaphylaxis (multi-system involvement or decreased BP by itself) and previous hospitalisation, the progression of symptoms can be quite fast.

The Importance of Food Diary

When recalling details, the patient's memory cannot always be relied upon. In addition, there's the inability to appropriately correlate the source and the symptoms caused. Overall, there's too much of a mix-and-match on the part of the patient when inquired about the details pertaining to the event. Hence, a food diary is more like a prospective study of the patient's allergic reaction to a particular food/s.

The food diary is a very important tool in the diagnosis of food allergies and consists of jotting down the patient's observations about their food intake and habits in the minutest details. This entails recording every item that the patient may have consumed before a reaction. This would include even innocuous items such as chewing gum, gelo, and chips.

If the details are recorded in the diary with utmost diligence and full interest, it can unravel an unrecognised link between food and the symptoms experienced by the patient. The flip side of this is that the patient can be obsessed with only food and not take non-food items into consideration, such as the environment, which too can sometimes cause a similar reaction. For example, lip swelling can be caused by dust mites which is an environmental factor.

A few pointers to keep in mind for a food diary:

1. The diary should be written in a simple and easy-to-understand manner.
2. Emphasis should be put on noting down the description of the reaction such as rashes, vomiting, tummy pain, diarrhoea, lip, eye swelling, etc.

3. The time gap between the events should also be noted. For example, how soon or late after eating a particular food did the reaction happen?
4. Apart from it, precise ingredients details and types of food eaten should also be noted. For example, in Indian cuisine, we need to differentiate between homemade masala and the ready-mix masala powder available in the market.

Elimination Diets

The strategy of eliminating food substances has double advantages. It can help in the diagnosis as well as have a therapeutic benefit.

- **Method**

  Only one food should be eliminated at a time and this is done for a period of at least two weeks. In addition, there shouldn't be other factors that provoke symptoms similar to a food allergy. Patients should avoid foods that are labelled as 'may contain' also. (Refer to Section 6, Chapter 2)

- **Limitation of elimination**

  The elimination process does not help much to diagnose food allergy, especially in the case of chronic disorders such as asthma or eczema. On completely eliminating milk with its substitutes such as soy formula or casein (alimental) or an elemental formula (neocate), an improvement in the condition of an infant would be highly suggestive of food allergy to cow's milk or other foods. But it can also be due to lactose intolerance or a non-IgE mediated food intolerance such as food protein-induced enterocolitis syndrome (FPIES). Thus, it is not a foolproof method of diagnosis and may subsequently require more diagnostic tools mentioned in the investigation chapter for a definitive confirmation.

Natural History of Food Hypersensitivity

After the diagnosis is done, the most concerning aspect is the outcome followed by the treatment. Hypersensitivity typically begins in the first year of life. The different foods will cause symptoms at different ages. Their chances of outgrowing are dependent on the food as shown in the table. In recent times, the component analysis of the allergenic food will scientifically estimate the probability of outgrowth and also of developing anaphylaxis. There could also be the possibility of subsequently developing other food allergies over time.

Food allergies in children may be viewed as a marker of atopic predisposition. It may coexist with other atopic conditions such as atopic dermatitis, allergic rhinitis, and asthma. Hence, such children should be considered at potential risk for future asthma and environmental allergy.

1. Egg
    - 60-80 per cent of infants with egg allergy become tolerant of eggs by 5 years of age as per our study with the age group of 1.5-2 years.

2. Milk and Soy
    - Enterocolitis
        - Vast majority become tolerant within 2 years.

- IgE mediated
  - Host A. 1994: Prospective study of milk hypersensitivity in children infancy through 3 years.
  - 50 per cent outgrow by age 1 year, 70 per cent by age 2 years, and 85 per cent by age 3 years.
  - 3-4 fold increase in the risk of developing asthma or eczema.
  - As per our study, we found that children outgrow the allergy by 2 years of age.

3. Peanuts and tree nuts allergies tend to persist into adult life.
4. Fish and shellfish allergies usually persist throughout life.

Prevention of Food Allergies

The best and non-controversial albeit way—yet not foolproof—of preventing allergies is exclusively breastfeeding for the first six months of the child's life. (Refer to Appendix 1, Chapter 1)

The other important measures are to avoid any form of processed foods, colourants, additives, preservatives, and any form of artificial foods, especially for pregnant and lactating mothers for the first two years. The American Academy of Paediatrics has been waxing and waning on the timing of the introduction of solids and the type of weaning foods. This aspect has been dealt with extensively in the chapter on traditional Indian weaning foods and junk foods.

Oral Allergy Syndrome/Food Pollen Allergy Syndrome

Oral allergy syndrome (OAS) is an allergy to one or more fresh fruits and vegetables. It is a common food-related allergy in adults and is also increasingly diagnosed in older children. Symptoms are often confined to the mouth and develop within a few minutes of eating the food. The allergy in such cases is mostly proteins in the fruit that are similar to those found in trees (especially birch tree), grass, or weed pollens that causes hay fever.

- **Symptoms**

  Symptoms include itchiness or tingling in the lips and mouth. Sometimes, local swelling of lips and tongue—also known as angioedema—might occur. Less common are urticaria (nettle rash) and abdominal pain. Anaphylaxis (wheezing or breathing problems) is uncommon, occurring in only 1 in 50 patients.

- **Why are symptoms typically confined to the mouth?**

  Unlike other food allergies, symptoms in OAS are usually limited to the mouth, lips, tongue, and throat because the proteins causing the allergic reaction are broken down by saliva and digestive juices in the stomach. Cooking food also destroys the proteins present in the food. People with OAS may therefore be able to eat cooked fruit such as apple pie but react to raw apples. Processed foods such as jam and canned fruits are also often tolerated.

- **Foods involved**

  Most people with OAS react to only 1-2 foods, although some may develop allergy symptoms to several foods. There is presently no way to predict who will develop a problem with a particular food. Children suffering from pollen-induced hay fever and associated food allergies can continue to eat all foods irrespective of their sensitisation, if it does not cause any clinical symptoms.

Pollens Cross-Reacting with Fruits, Vegetables, and Nuts

Tree pollens (alder and birch)	Apple, cherry, carrot, peach, peas, beans, pear plum, potato, strawberry, tomato, almonds, hazelnuts, walnuts, coriander, fennel, parsley, peanut, soybean, and sunflower.
Grass pollen	Kiwi, melon, peas, potato, tomato, and peanut.
Mugwort pollen	Apples, carrot, celery, melon, onion, peach, pepper, tomato, basil, dill, fennel, mustard, oregano, parsley, pepper, and thyme.

Are Allergy Tests Useful?

Pollen skin tests may be considered if there are hay fever symptoms (sneezing and itchy or runny nose and eyes). There is often no reaction to standard skin testing solutions as the proteins (allergens) are destroyed in the process of producing the test solutions, just as they are in cooking. Skin testing by using fresh food for prick-to-prick tests and blood allergy tests to specific protein components of the food may support the diagnosis.

Foods can be safely tested at home by touching a little of the fresh food to the lip. If there is no tingling, itchiness, or swelling, then a bite may be taken after which the food should be chewed and spat out. If the patient is allergic, symptoms should occur within 15 minutes. If there are symptoms like swelling, wheezing, or abdominal pain, then one should test foods only after seeking medical advice.

Treatment

Raw foods causing troublesome symptoms should be avoided. Lightly cooked foods (dishes that include stir-fried vegetables or steamed/poached fruits or vegetables) can usually be tolerated, but if they also cause a reaction, they should also be avoided as well. If symptoms are more extensive and not confined to the mouth, specialist advice should be sought. Symptoms usually respond to rinsing the mouth and then taking a dose of antihistamine. As anaphylaxis is unlikely, injectable adrenaline devices are not usually necessary.

Case Scenario

A 10-month-old NRI girl with atopic dermatitis visited my clinic. She was bottle-fed in the first month and then strictly breastfed. She was weaned at 6 months onto a strict vegetarian diet of pulses, wheat, rice, vegetables, and occasionally fruits. Both mother and baby were off milk completely since the baby had reacted adversely to milk (severe rash and vomiting). The results were as follows:

Allergen	Specific IgE	Skin Prick Test
Peanut	>100 kUA/1	5mm
Almond	89.40	3 mm
Cashew nut	>100	8 mm
Hazelnut	>100	Not Tested
Pista	>100	8 mm
Walnut	67.70	Not Tested
Kabuli Chana	>100	Not Tested
Gluten/Wheat	91	Nil
Soya	Not Tested	3 mm
Milk	51	Not Tested

This child was advised to continue taking wheat, soya, and almond since she was consuming them freely despite positive results. Milk was stopped because of previous adverse reactions, and she was advised to rechallenge after one year. The tree nuts, peanuts, and chana were stopped because of strong positivity on blood and skin prick testing.

Salient Points

- Food allergy and food intolerance have to be differentiated.
- Diagnosis is mainly by clinical history, appropriate diagnostic test (SPT or immunoassay for specific IgE), and supervised food challenge, aided with/out food diary and elimination diets.
- Discussion with patients and their families will help them deal with reactions and enable them to have an anaphylaxis action plan, if required.
- Food intolerance is more common in our country as compared to food allergy.
- General public should be made aware of oral allergy syndrome.

4

Non-IgE Mediated Food Allergy

The chapter discusses food intolerance and other food disorders which are not IgE mediated but are of equal importance as there are no proper diagnostic tests for the same and impact the growth of the affected children.

Introduction

The allergy terminologies are not well-known by general public which leads to misunderstanding. In the context of food allergy, correct diagnosis is possible with:

1. A good clinical history.
2. Demonstration of sensitisation to in vivo and/or in vitro tests to prove underlying mechanism and possibly, the aetiology.

The mechanism of non-IgE mediated food allergy is not well understood. Although the immune system is presumed to be involved, IgE antibodies are not associated with this condition and hence the term 'non-IgE mediated' food allergy. This term is an umbrella term for a range of gastrointestinal food allergies that affect the full or partial length of the gut.

Non-IgE Mediated Food Allergic Disorders

In this case, food allergy is also linked to manifestations of delayed hypersensitivity, partial IgE-mediated, and partial non-IgE-mediated. It is implicated in eosinophilic esophagitis, eosinophilic gastritis, gastroenteritis, food protein-induced enterocolitis syndrome, and allergic proctocolitis.

1. **Food protein–induced enter colitis syndrome (FPIES)**

   This disorder typically affects infants and there are 2 types of it: acute and chronic. The chronic forms manifest as vomiting, diarrhoea, failure to thrive, and in severe cases, lethargy and malnutrition. In the acute case, the presentation or re-introduction of eliminated food can result in vomiting, loose stools, and decreased blood pressure with dehydration (especially in younger babies) resembling acute gastroenteritis. This may lead to the condition being very often missed and is instead, often treated as an infection. In contrast to an IgE mediated food allergic reaction, there will be no rash and the patient will not respond to anti-allergic medication including adrenaline.

   This disorder is often associated with cow's milk, soy, oat, wheat, and less commonly with rice or lentils. Blood test and skin prick test are usually negative for suspected foods in general but can occur concomitantly with IgE mediated food allergies also.

2. **Food protein-induced allergic proctocolitis (FPIAP)**

FPIAP typically happens in the first few months of the child's life and results in blood in the stools. It is a benign condition affecting about 50-60 per cent of babies being breastfed and the rest in formula-fed babies. Some of the uncommon presentations include failure to thrive with anaemia. The treatment for this disorder includes avoidance of the incriminating food for the baby and mother too, if she is breastfeeding.

3. **Food-induced pulmonary hemosiderosis (Heiner's Syndrome)**

It is a rare syndrome, affecting infants and young children, and is characterised by recurrent episodes of pneumonia associated with lung infiltrates, hemosiderosis, gastrointestinal blood loss, iron deficiency, anaemia, and failure to thrive. The condition is mainly attributed to cow's milk with the immunologic mechanism being poorly defined.

Mixed-IgE and Non-IgE Reactions

1. **Atopic Dermatitis**

It is a mixed disorder and at least 30-40 per cent of infants and toddlers with atopic eczema have concomitant food allergy, especially in severe cases. Among foods that cause acute exacerbations in these patients, egg is the most common allergic food. Proper diagnosis and counselling regarding scientific elimination of the offending food allergen lead to improvement of the skin issues in most of these cases. However, it must be emphasised that the elimination of the allergic food will decrease the exacerbation but not have much effect on the disappearance of the atopic disease.

2. Allergic Eosinophilic Oesophagitis (EoE)

This condition in children can lead to a variety of non-specific symptoms like nausea, vomiting, heartburn, and failure to thrive. Teenagers and adults are more likely to have dysphagia and episodes of food impaction. Some important pointers regarding EoE include:

i. Eighty per cent of patients with eosinophilic esophagitis have symptoms similar to gastroesophageal reflux, which are refractory to anti-reflux therapy. In the case of infants, the vomitus often contains stringy mucus, similar to egg albumin.

ii. Patients may also show symptoms such as food refusal, dysphagia, food impaction, or abdominal pain. Food-induced IgE mediated allergy has been implicated in the pathogenesis in some patients.

iii. In some cases of eosinophilic esophagitis, there may be a childhood subclinical disease or a silent chronic inflammation which remains unrecognised and undiagnosed for years.

3. **Allergic Eosinophilic Gastritis**

   For this disorder, the mechanism remains unknown, even though both IgE and non-IgE mediated mechanisms have been hypothesised. Clinical presentation includes nausea and vomiting after ingestion of food, tummy pain, and diarrhoea, mainly reported as steatorrhea, weight loss in young-adults, and failure to thrive in young children.

How Does Non-IgE Mediated Food Allergy Differ from IgE Mediated Food Allergy?

Non-IgE mediated food allergy is less well understood than IgE mediated food allergy. As the symptoms are usually delayed as compared to IgE mediated food allergy, it is more difficult to diagnose and correlate with the clinical symptoms and the offending food.

The method diagnosis of non-Ige mediated food allergy consists of elimination and challenge methods. The lack of accurate diagnostic tests further compounds the problem. The most common causative foods for non-IgE mediated food allergies are cow's milk and soy proteins in infants and wheat in older children. Non-IgE food allergies are very rarely life-threatening because they do not result in anaphylaxis, unlike IgE mediated food allergies.

What Are the Common Symptoms for Non-IgE Mediated Food Allergy?

Common symptoms include abdominal discomfort, vomiting, and diarrhoea. In some patients, constipation or colic can be the presenting symptom. The symptoms often take longer to develop (hours to days) rather than those of IgE mediated food allergies, which frequently occur within a few minutes to two hours following the offending food ingestion.

How Is Non-IgE Mediated Food Allergy Diagnosed?

Unlike IgE mediated food allergy, there are no blood or skin tests which have proved useful in general medical practice. Hence, the diagnosis is mainly based on the history and may be confirmed by observing that the symptoms improve when the suspected food is removed from the diet and return when the food is reintroduced into the diet. This process can take a number of weeks or months to complete properly and is termed the eliminate-rechallenge test. The re-challenge aspect of the test is very important to confirm the link between the offending food and symptoms since symptoms can resolve by chance.

Most clinicians recommend that the food be removed for 2-4 weeks. If symptoms resolve, then the food is gradually reintroduced to assess whether symptoms recur. Only one food type at a time is removed. If more than one food type is removed, it is recommended that a dietician trained in allergy elimination diets is involved in the care of the patient.

Can Non-IgE Mediated and IgE Mediated Food Allergy Occur in the Same Individual?

Yes, children can have both types of food allergies. This can be the situation particularly in children with severe eczema.

Can Children Grow Out of Non-IgE Mediated Food Allergy?

Yes, but there is very less information on the time involved in children as well as adults who grow out of non-IgE mediated food allergy.

Are There Any Allergy Tests for Non-IgE Mediated Food Allergy?

There are no blood or skin allergy tests that can accurately diagnose the issue. The diagnoses are established by the removal of the suspected food(s) which is followed by a rechallenge test, if the symptoms improve. Once a diagnosis is established, the main step in treatment is avoidance of the relevant food.

Case Scenario

This case concerns a 5-month-old boy who had been previously well and exclusively breastfed. At the age of 4 months, he was introduced to the cow's milk formula. Two weeks after, he was fed the formula for the second time and 2 hours later, he developed repetitive vomiting and hypotensive with oliguria and looked lethargic. Then, the child had severe dehydration and was tachycardic and tachypnoeic. His weight was less than the third centile. He was admitted and sent for further investigation.

He was rehydrated and stabilised and investigations revealed leucocytosis, hyponatraemia, and lactic acidosis. The specific IgE for milk was negative. Metabolic and infectious problems were excluded.

Based on the clinical results, clinical suspicion of FPIES was quite high. Cow's milk formula was eliminated from the diet of the baby and he was started on amino acid formula which was well tolerated, and symptoms abated over a period of few days. The weight gradually improved to the twenty-fifth centile after a period of 6-8 weeks.

Salient Points

- Common symptoms include abdominal discomfort, vomiting, and diarrhoea; rash is not present.
- In some cases, constipation or colic can be the presenting symptoms along with failure to gain weight.
- The symptoms often take longer to develop (hours to days) rather than those of IgE mediated food allergies which frequently occur within 5-30 minutes following food ingestion.

5

Systemic Manifestations of Food Allergies

The chapter briefly discusses the effects of food allergies on the different systems, the importance of recognising the symptoms, and their subsequent management.

Introduction

As we have discussed, food allergy is an adverse immunologic reaction to certain foods, whereby the immune system attacks certain food proteins, which are usually harmless to the majority of the population. Generally, food allergy does not affect a single organ system nor is it a single disease. This shows that a small protein content of a single food can cause different symptoms in different individuals. Certain foods like peanuts and tree nuts are likely to cause severe systemic allergic reactions like anaphylaxis, which can be fatal, but some foods like wheat is associated with gastrointestinal diseases. Various factors can influence this spectrum of clinical systemic manifestations of food allergy like the atopic predisposition, immune deregulation, inherent property of the foods ingested, and preexisting diseases like asthma.

Some of the common IgE mediated, immediate food allergy reactions are as follows:

1. Skin
    - Urticaria
    - Angioedema
2. Respiratory
    - Asthma, wheezing, and cough
    - Rhino conjunctivitis or laryngeal oedema
3. Gastrointestinal
    - Vomiting
    - Diarrhoea
    - Colic
    - Oral allergy syndrome
4. Cardiovascular
    - Hypotension
5. Systemic
    - Anaphylaxis

Some of the common non-IgE mediated or mixed-type symptoms of CMPA are as follows:

1. Skin
    - Atopic dermatitis
2. Gastrointestinal
    - Eosinophilic oesophagitis (feeding difficulties, gastroesophageal reflux disease, abdominal pain, and dysphagia)
    - Food protein enteropathy
    - Food protein-induced enterocolitis (failure to thrive, blood in stools, and sepsis-like picture in acute presentation with pallor, vomiting, and diarrhoea)

- Food protein-induced proctocolitis (normal growth with mild rectal bleeding)
- Gastro-oesophageal reflux
- Chronic diarrhoea or constipation
- Iron deficiency (anaemia)

3. Respiratory
    - Heiner Syndrome (pulmonary hemosiderosis)

Note: Even if the initial contact with the food is in the gastrointestinal tract, there are various manifestations of the allergy in different organs. Studies demonstrate that children with atopic dermatitis had positive double-blinded food challenges, which mainly affected gastrointestinal system along with skin manifestations.

Dermatological Manifestations

Several skin manifestations are caused by food allergies. Most of these disorders are mediated by allergen-specific IgE that is bound to FcRe receptors on mast cells in the blood. Typical manifestations are urticaria and angioedema in the majority of the cases. Overall, food allergy contributes to approximately 25-30 per cent of acute urticaria.

Atopic eczema is a chronic condition of the skin with acute exacerbation, along with underlying T cell response to the ingested protein, associated with food-specific IgE antibodies. Atopic dermatitis is associated with food allergy in one-third of children and it ranges from moderate to severe atopic dermatitis.

Skin manifestations can also be in the form of dermatitis herpetiformis, where the lesions are distributed over the extensor surfaces of the elbows, knees, and buttocks. It is associated with specific sensitivity to gluten without the involvement of the IgE.

The mainstay of treatment of atopic dermatitis is moisturisers besides a host of other topical agents including steroids and immunomodulators like tacrolimus.

Gastrointestinal Tract

Many gastrointestinal allergic diseases additionally have some kind of systemic involvement. Traditionally, symptoms involving only GI symptoms may not be truly considered systemic involvement, but it could be a delayed manifestation/mixed cell disorder like FPIEs or proctocolitis syndrome.

Initial GI symptoms of vomiting and abdominal pain could progress to lethargy, dehydration, acidosis, and decreased blood pressure, which can be mistaken many a time as sepsis/bacterial infection and treated accordingly.

Oral Allergy Syndrome (OAS) is a local contact reaction, mediated by a specific IgE antibody and is associated with itching, uneasiness, and swelling of the mouth. It is usually seen in patients with allergic rhinitis and pollen sensitivities. Also, this syndrome is triggered by proteins found in fresh fruits and vegetables, which cross-react with pollens to which the patient may have been sensitised. The patients can often tolerate the same fruits and vegetables in the cooked form without any systemic manifestations. In a small subset of patients, it can be associated with vomiting and diarrhoea.

In patients with non-IgE mediated FA, clinical presentations are not straightforward and can be varied, depending on many factors.

Patients with celiac disease have lower GI symptoms, which are mainly caused by gluten hypersensitivity, though it is not a true food allergy. It is mainly caused by damage to the intestinal villi by the gluten in wheat. Also, in such cases, allergy tests are always negative.

On similar lines, food protein enteropathy occurring secondary to cow's milk protein is a transient health issue in the first year of life and doesn't persist into late childhood on most occasions. On the other hand, allergic eosinophilic gastroenteritis is a more persistent and serious medical condition, triggered by various foods. It affects different parts of the GI system, leading to chronic issues and affects the quality of life of patients.

Respiratory System

In India, foods are commonly thought to be the cause of respiratory symptoms, and this leads to unnecessary avoidance of certain foods. But more often than not, this is not the case and let's see the reason why.

Food allergy symptoms are elicited in the upper and lower respiratory symptoms, in conjunction with other systemic symptoms like the skin and GI system among others. Isolated nasal symptoms are very uncommon presentations of food allergic reactions. The symptoms manifested are more likely due to the chemicals in the food like histamine which have an irritant effect on the denuded mucosa. It's like adding insult to injury akin to applying chilli powder on abraded skin.

Another point to note is that asthma is not a common manifestation of food allergy. However, it is often triggered, during the severe systemic allergic manifestation. Uncontrolled asthma is a risk factor for fatal food anaphylaxis. Food allergy may increase the airway sensitivity towards foods in susceptible individuals. These reactions are mainly mediated by food-specific IgE.

Heiner Syndrome is a pulmonary manifestation of food allergy which is not IgE mediated. It is mainly associated in infancy with the reaction of protein in the cow's milk with the immune system, mediated mainly by IgE. Clinical manifestations include pulmonary infiltrates and hemosiderosis, anaemia, failure to thrive, and recurrent pneumonia. Luckily, it is one of the rarer presentations of food allergy in children.

Factors that Determine Clinical Expression of Food Allergy

A variety of factors determine the clinical expression of food allergy like genetic predisposition, target organ reactivity, protein absorption, degree of immune response, route of allergen exposure, quantity ingested, environmental exposure, and the type of immune response to the allergen. Thus, we can see that several variables contribute to how the systemic manifestations of the food allergy occur.

Case Scenario

Refer to the case in the next chapter on anaphylaxis.

Salient Points

- Systemic symptoms occur when an allergic reaction progresses from a single organ system (most commonly the skin) to include at least one other system.
- Symptoms often include the following: redness, swelling, blistering, itching, hives and rashes, shortness of breath, and exacerbation of eczema among others.
- Food causing respiratory symptoms without any other symptoms is very uncommon and is mostly due to a non-allergic cause.

6

Acute and Life-Threatening Allergies—Anaphylaxis

This is the most important aspect of food allergy and a major concern because it can cause death if untreated. This chapter emphasises the magnitude of the same and the importance of appropriately treating it, especially in a country like India where it is under-diagnosed due to a lack of awareness among doctors and the general public alike.

Introduction

The word anaphylaxis was first coined by Richet in the year 1902 and it means 'without protection' ('ana'—without and 'phylaxis'—protection). It is a severe form of an allergic reaction which can be fatal, if not recognised and treated appropriately.

Common Allergens Known to Cause Anaphylaxis

The details are as follows:

- Drugs like penicillin, sulphonamides, vancomycin, and other parenteral and oral medications as well as intravenous radiocontrast medications.
- Foods such as peanuts/groundnuts, fish, legumes, milk, and eggs.

- Stinging insect bites by bees, fire ants, and wasps among others.
- Latex allergy.
- Idiopathic.

The Mechanism of Anaphylaxis

A susceptible child on initial contact with an allergen (sensitising dose) is sensitised and on re-exposure to the same allergen (shocking dose) develops anaphylaxis. The mechanism of anaphylaxis is almost similar to bronchial asthma, except for a few differences. The primary mediators in anaphylaxis are histamine, and the target organs are the skin, mucous membranes, and airway, whereas in asthma, the primary mediators are mainly leukotrienes, and the target organ is the lung.

The exposure of a susceptible child to the incriminating allergen results in the allergen binding to the antigen-specific IgE. This leads to degranulation of mast cells and basophils, resulting in sudden and increased release of inflammatory mediators of anaphylaxis.

Clinical Features of Anaphylaxis

In the vast majority of cases, the skin and mucous membrane are involved, which are the main target organs for anaphylaxis. Skin manifestations could be generalised hives with or without angioedema. Even a documented hypotension or respiratory compromise, in the absence of skin manifestations can be a presentation of anaphylaxis. Generally, it is life-threatening and can involve laryngospasm, hypotension, and shock, which can result in death due to complete airway obstruction.

Diagnosis

The diagnosis of anaphylaxis is strictly clinical but in cases of injected allergen, one can do a blood mast cell tryptase level provided the blood was collected within 6 hours of the attack. Due to the risks and fatalities associated with the above allergies, it is imperative that one should consult an allergist at the earliest opportunity to identify the allergen, preferably, through a skin prick test and start the suitable treatment.

The NIAID (National Institute of Allergy and Infectious Diseases) in Washington has laid down guidelines for the diagnosis of anaphylaxis (table given on next page). These are only guidelines to make a diagnosis but what is most important is having a degree of suspicion about anaphylaxis. There are many co-factors which can aggravate or compound the whole situation. Poorly controlled asthma or allergic rhinitis, exercise, alcohol, and some drugs such as non-steroidal anti-inflammatory, and angiotensin-converting enzyme inhibitors are co-factors which can predispose to more severe allergic reactions.

Diagnostic Clinical Criteria for Anaphylaxis (NIAID Guidelines)

Anaphylaxis is highly likely when any one of the following three criteria is fulfilled: 1. Acute onset of an illness (minutes to several hours) with the involvement of the skin, mucosal tissue, or both (example, generalised urticaria, itching or flushing, and swollen lips, tongue, and uvula). AND at least one of the following: a. Respiratory compromise (example, dyspnoea, wheeze-bronchospasm, stridor, reduced PEF, and hypoxemia). b. Reduced blood pressure or associated symptoms of end-organ dysfunction (example hypotonia, collapse, syncope, and incontinence).
2. Two or more of the following occur rapidly after exposure to a likely allergen for that patient (minutes to several hours). a. Involvement of the skin-mucosal tissue (example generalised urticaria, itch-flush, swollen lips, tongue, and uvula). b. Respiratory compromise (example dyspnoea, wheeze-bronchospasm, stridor, reduced PEF, and hypoxemia). c. Reduced blood pressure or associated

symptoms (example hypotonic, collapse, syncope, and incontinence).

d. Persistent gastrointestinal symptoms (example crampy abdominal pain and vomiting).

3. Reduced blood pressure after exposure to a known allergen for that patient (minutes to several hours).

   a. Infants and children: low systolic blood pressure (age-specific) or greater than 30 per cent decrease in systolic blood pressure.

   b. Adults: systolic blood pressure of less than 90 mm Hg or greater than 30 per cent decrease from that person's baseline.

Treatment

Anaphylaxis and anaphylactic shock must always be treated as a medical emergency.

1. A: Airway patency and if there is a compromise due to laryngeal swelling or bag and mask ventilation, and if required cricothyrotomy may be lifesaving.
2. B: Maintain breathing and administer oxygen to keep saturation>90.
3. C: Maintain circulation. Patients with shock may require fluid resuscitation with normal saline or ringer lactate.

Specific treatment for anaphylaxis:

1. Adrenaline
2. Antihistamines
3. Steroids

Let's explore all these pointers in detail.

Adrenaline

This is the first drug of choice for the systemic manifestation of anaphylaxis and is the only lifesaving drug for an anaphylactic shock.

i. Adrenaline rapidly reverses the airway compromise, relieving laryngeal swelling and bronchospasm.
ii. It increases and maintains blood pressure and by acting on beta receptors, it increases myocardial contractility, heart rate, and coronary perfusion.
iii. Adrenaline is a physiological antagonist of histamine and therefore offers quick relief of urticaria, angioedema, and laryngeal swelling of anaphylaxis.

- **Dose and Route**

i. 0.01ml/kg (1:10000) intramuscular, most of the patients will respond to the first dose.
ii. If still no response in 15 minutes, give 2nd dose of 0.01ml /kg (1:1000) intramuscular.
iii. If there is still no response and the child is in shock, start IV infusion at the rate of 0.1 to 1 microgram/kg/min till the desired response.

- **Caution**

  Rapid infusion may cause death from cardiac arrhythmias. Hence always avoid intravenous outside an ICU setting even in the presence of an intravenous line.

Antihistamines

They effectively block histamine-induced triple response like wheal, flare, and itch (urticaria, itching, and angio-oedema). It acts as an adjunctive treatment to adrenaline. The best antihistamine in children is 2nd generation non-sedating antihistamines like cetirizine, fexofenadine, or bilastine.

Steroids

Steroids have a role in reversing bronchospasm and cutaneous effects of anaphylaxis. They also prevent or ameliorate the biphasic or relapse phenomenon of anaphylaxis.

i. Drug prednisolone, oral, 1mg/kg/day QID for less form for 2-3 days.
ii. For the severe form, IV methyl prednisone, 1-2mg /kg IV, every 6 hours.

Monitoring

All patients with anaphylaxis should be monitored till complete resolution of symptoms and there is no recurrence of symptoms for at least 24 hours.

Prevention

1. **Patient Education**
   The key to prevention is avoidance. Identify and avoid exposure to the inciting agents.

2. **Allergy Testing**
   When the causative agent is not known, allergy testing may help to identify the agent and help in desensitisation. If a skin prick test is being done then it should be delayed for six weeks.

Medicolegal Pitfalls

Claims for medical negligence related to anaphylaxis are not uncommon. Some of the common medicolegal pitfalls have been given below:

1. Failure to consider the diagnosis in patients with unexplained shock or syncope.
2. Administration/prescription of the drug to which the patient is allergic.
3. Failure to warn the patient about the preventive measures.
4. Failure to appreciate the potentially severe nature of symptoms.

Case Study

Rucha, a 13-year-old girl, had peanut allergy and asthma since two-and-a-half years of age. Her SPT was positive for peanuts and an EpiPen (adrenaline injection) was prescribed. She seemed lost on her follow up and was being managed by her family physician. In August 2011, she ate chicken tikka masala in a cafe. After returning from a holiday, she ordered a takeaway. She reassured her mother that she has eaten that dish earlier with no reaction. On eating the delivered food, she felt a tingling sensation, and shortness of breath and also got swollen lips within 15 minutes. She didn't have EpiPen with her and so, a salbutamol inhaler and antihistamine were given by her mother and the ambulance was also called.

On arrival, the paramedics gave adrenaline 0.5mg IM (left deltoid). The ambulance crew felt Rucha had a severe allergic reaction and so they administered salbutamol neb, IV chlorpheniramine, and then adrenaline 0.5mg IM (left Deltoid) was given and IV fluids were started. She showed marked clinical improvement and became fully conscious. She was able to talk in sentences and thus, the ambulance took her to a tertiary care centre.

Rucha was admitted in the accident and emergency department. She was fully conscious with swollen lips and tongue and her SpO2 was 98 per cent on 10L/minute oxygen and all vitals were normal. Hydrocortisone 200 mg IV, salbutamol, ipratropium nebulisation, and adrenaline 0.5mg IM were given. She showed further improvement clinically and was referred to the paediatric team for admission.

Her ECG and chest X-ray were normal and her SpO2 was 100 per cent on 10L/min of oxygen with normal vitals, when she suddenly had shortness of breath. She felt warm and irritable, and her lips and tongue started swelling again with throat pain and she couldn't breathe. Adrenaline 0.5mg IM was given immediately and the crash team was called in. There was a further deterioration of SpO2 80-85 per cent on 10L/min O2 after which Rucha collapsed with a big vomit.

Resuscitation was initiated, and she was intubated by

the consultant anaesthetist. She showed some improvement initially and her SpO2 went upwards of 92 per cent. But over the next 10-15 minutes, she was deteriorating further. In spite of all the best internationally recommended measures, CPR was unsuccessful. Her serum tryptase levels were normal.

A post-mortem examination showed lips and tongue swelling, prominent laryngeal oedema, mucous plugging of small airways with prominent oedema, and eosinophilic infiltration. The tikka masala recipe contained mixed nuts which are 90 per cent peanuts and 10 per cent almond.

Pictorial Representation of Anaphylaxis Presentation

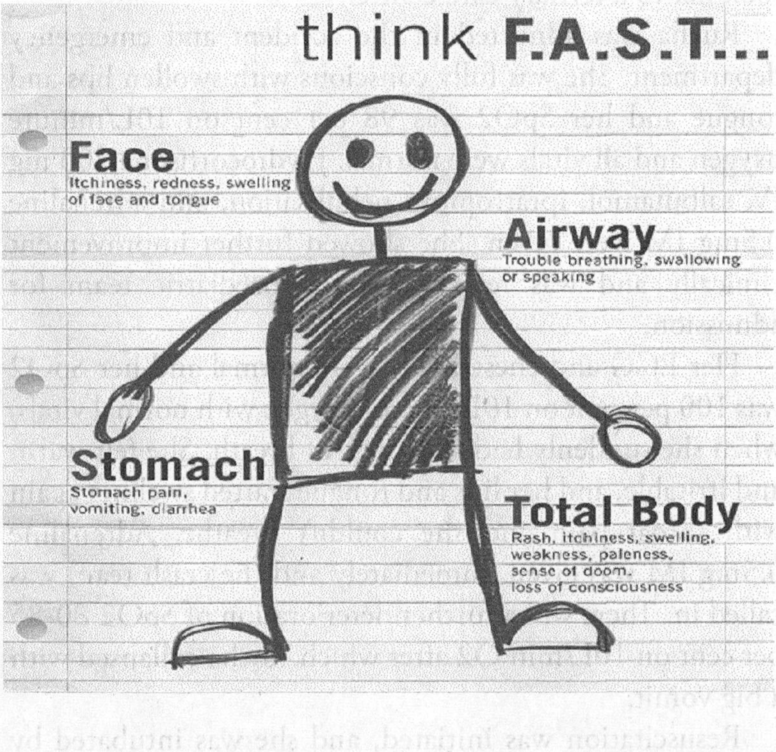

Salient Points

- Anaphylaxis is a severe, systemic hypersensitivity reaction that is rapid in onset.
- It is characterised by life-threatening airway, breathing, and/or circulatory problems, which are usually associated with skin and mucosal changes.
- This problem is under-diagnosed and under-treated both by medical professionals and the general public alike.
- Intramuscular epinephrine is the mainstay of treatment for anaphylaxis.

7
Approach to Food Allergies

'There is nothing more deceptive than obvious fact.'
—Sherlock Holmes

This quote captures an essential truth about food allergies that what you see and hear need not be the true food allergy and we are going the explore the same in this chapter.

Introduction

Food allergy is an ever-evolving field with no clear boundaries. And due to this, many adverse food reactions are mistakenly labelled as food allergies. Therefore, it is important to educate the healthcare providers, patients, and their families so that they can properly recognise, appropriately diagnose, and manage issues.

Many factors, both known and unknown, contribute to the dynamics of FA all around the world. Taking the example of peanut/groundnut allergy or sensitisation, we find that it has increased in the developed world, in contrast to the low level of allergy to groundnuts in South and East Asia regions (India, China, Israel, etc.) where the consumption is far higher. Studies have demonstrated that the introduction of highly allergenic food in the form of age-appropriate weaning foods early in life may have contributed to the low level of allergy/sensitisation in these regions.

Another possible factor contributing to the prevalence of an allergy in a region is the method of preparation. In the West, peanuts are predominantly roasted while in East and South-East Asia, it is boiled. Many environmental and lifestyle factors like animal and microbiota exposure, number of siblings, time spent outdoors, exposure to environmental tobacco smoke, ingestion of processed foods, obesity, and repeated antibiotic use in the first year of life among others have contributed to this changing picture along with genetic predisposition. Apart from it, there are also many unknown factors, which are not yet fully understood, that play a crucial role in the prevalence of allergies. For example, the food intake is also a contributing factor in the case of pregnant and lactating mothers.

And when it comes to managing a food allergy, it may seem that avoiding a particular food item is a good strategy, but it is easier said than done for the patient. Therefore, we must be absolutely thorough in our approach with a patient in the case of a suspected food allergy.

Most of the population is able to tolerate major food allergens. These allergens are essentially weak and are unable to trigger the immune system because of various protective factors. Our gastrointestinal system has a unique defence in place and glycocalyx is one of them. It acts as a sealing agent for the surface epithelia and traps food particles from getting absorbed in the immunologically stable form.

A few questions to be asked in the case of a food allergy are as follows:

1. How soon did the symptoms occur after eating the food?

2. Do the symptoms recur each time after eating the food in question?
3. What were the symptoms after the ingestion of food?
4. Does eating the food in cooked form cause any symptoms?
5. Are there any concomitant medications being taken during the occurrence of allergic symptoms?

Diagnosis

Identifying the patient with a food allergy can be challenging, as symptoms may be non-specific and causality difficult to establish. Hence, a thorough history is needed to guide further testing and exclude alternative diagnoses. Relevant factors to assess include symptoms and suspected allergen, number of occurrences, the quantity of food ingested, method of food preparation, relationship to exercise, relationship to alcohol and painkiller ingestion, duration of symptoms, presence of symptoms without food ingestion, and proximity of symptoms to exposure.

Another aspect to consider is how much time it takes for the symptoms to show up. IgE mediated food allergies typically present itself within minutes of ingestion, whereas food intolerances may show up hours later. Eczema exacerbation may be seen hours after ingestion of a food allergen.

An elimination diet followed by reintroduction or provocation can be considered in order to establish a correlative relationship. This is different from an oral challenge, which is allergist-guided and has been covered in the later chapters. Urticaria rashes typically occur in an IgE mediated reaction and therefore would occur within an hour or two of the food ingestion. Also, food as an etiology is very rare in chronic urticaria.

FA should be considered in patients with IgE mediated symptoms, adults with eosinophilic esophagitis (EoE), and select older children with moderate to severe atopic dermatitis. There is no evidence suggesting that the prevalence of food allergy is higher in patients with celiac disease. When attempting to distinguish between a food allergy and food intolerance, respiratory, skin, eye, and cardiovascular symptoms are more suggestive of an allergic process and should prompt further workup. Once a food allergy is suspected by history, patients should be referred to an allergist well-versed with food allergy.

Case Scenario

A 60-year-old female came to me complaining that she had rashes when she would eat seafood. However, the history of fish allergy was very vague. There was no definite history of allergy after eating various types of fish and we just could not pin it down to fish since she had a reaction to a saltwater fish on mere exposure to the fumes. Also, on her next consumption of seawater and freshwater fish, she didn't get any reaction. She also had episodes of getting rashes sometimes after swimming irrespective of whether the water was chlorinated or not.

She was tested for different fishes and common allergens including wheat. All were negative on SPT. We challenged her with fish in a hospital setting. It too came out negative.

On further and detailed questioning, which was indeed time-consuming, we found that whenever she got rash, there was a consumption of wheat. On most occasions, it was accompanied by excessive physical activity. On one occasion, there was no physical activity but she simultaneously consumed aspirin.

We did a component analysis of wheat and she was positive for Omega 5-Gliadin. This component is a member of the gliadin family and can cause wheat dependant, exercise-induced anaphylaxis (WDEIA). On consumption of wheat, there was no reaction unless it was followed by excessive activity, including having a bath or with co-factors such as aspirin.

Salient Points

- Keep a food diary when symptoms are not attributable to a detailed history.
- Keep a tab on regular medication usage, any alcohol consumption, or exercise routine, if contributing to the symptoms.
- Do not avoid food unnecessarily without medical supervision.
- Do not get a blood test done on your own and without doctor's advice.

Section III
DIAGNOSIS

1
Laboratory Diagnosis of Allergic Diseases

Patients and even doctors have poor knowledge of various laboratory tests for allergies. This chapter covers the prominent tests and their importance in addition to the latest methods to diagnose the allergen. It also explains how to overcome and manage food allergies and how the laboratory can help with outgrowing the disease.

Introduction

Diagnosis of allergic disorders is simply . . . clinical. The clinical aspect is emphasised since a well-taken history of the patient would sufficiently help to diagnose allergic diseases. Thus, the test only has a secondary role in making the diagnosis of an allergic disorder and is more for affirming or refuting the clinical diagnosis. The test may support the clinical diagnosis but should not be used as a screening test. Allergy tests can sometimes be omitted if a thorough medical history check of the patient is conducted by a knowledgeable clinician with input from the family.

How Is Allergy Testing Done?

The determination of the allergen starts with a meticulous analysis of the patient's history followed by either a skin test or a blood test for the specific IgE. An estimate of the total IgE present is not a good predictor of allergies in children. Positive allergy test results indicate sensitisation or atopy, but they are not equivalent to clinical allergy. This means that a child can have a positive allergen test indicating that he is atopic to that allergen, but it doesn't confirm that the same allergen is responsible for his symptoms. In simple terms, a child with positive allergy tests may have no clinical illness when exposed to the allergen. Thereby highlighting the importance of meticulous examination and analysis of the patient's history in order to narrow down the suspected allergens list and then carry out specific allergen tests rather than ordering a battery of tests.

Another point to note here is that positive allergy testing has no correlation with the severity of the allergic state. Total serum IgE can be raised in one-third of the population and therefore is not a measure of clinical allergy. IgE can be particularly high in a number of other conditions, particularly in:

- Atopic dermatitis
- Parasitic infections
- Neoplastic diseases
- Immunodeficiency diseases

I find many patients coming to the clinic with a preconditioned diagnosis of allergy, because either their referring doctor has told them about the abnormal levels of non-specific IgE or the patient has noticed the elevated levels themselves. But the fact is that total non-specific IgE levels are generally inconsequential and patients are just misled by these values. A specific IgE for an allergen level has a greater value when it comes to a more precise diagnosis of the allergy. But there is one more thing to know here. Total IgE or specific IgE are usually not helpful for monitoring disease activity as levels may remain high, even after the patient has become tolerant to the allergen. Hence, the doctors as well as the patients have to take into account all the factors mentioned here.

Another factor to consider when it comes to allergy diagnosis is the growth in general awareness about food allergies. The laws mandating labelling and prevention campaigns have also contributed to a growing awareness of food allergy. The downside of this aspect is that it leads people to attribute many symptoms to food allergy without seeking confirmation as well as to the increased use of IgE testing with the inevitable false-positive results.

***

Anaphylaxis Diagnosis

In the case of anaphylaxis, serum mast cell tryptase will be elevated only if the route of entry of the allergen is by the parenteral route, i.e., as an injected drug or an insect bite. An ingested allergen causing anaphylaxis will not necessarily elevate the mast cell tryptase levels. Thus, it is important that the sample is collected within 2-3 hours of the incidence. It is also advisable to repeat the levels 12 hours after the initial sample to demonstrate the declining trend of the values. The case study in the chapter 'Anaphylaxis' is an indicator of normal mast cell tryptase in food allergy.

Other Tests Available to Identify the Allergens

- Skin Prick Test (SPT) and Intradermal Test
- Oral Food Challenge Test

Factors Helping in Deciding a Test

The broad factors are as follows:

1. **Patient Related**

   The skin condition in eczema and urticaria is sometimes not conducive for SPT allergy testing especially if the disease is extensive or the skin is very greasy. Very young children, sometimes, in spite of the best counselling, would not allow for skin testing. In order to do the skin prick test, the patient should be off antihistamines such as hydroxyzine or chlorpheniramine (Avil) for at least 5 days and off second-generation antihistamines such as cetirizine and similar ones for at least 7 days. If the patient cannot be without antihistamines, then there is no option other than doing a blood test. Also, unlike a blood test, skin prick tests are often cheaper, more reliable, and provide an immediate result.

2. **Physician Related**

   If the physician is rather uncomfortable doing the skin prick test or if he is not familiar with the test, then the blood test would be recommended.

3. **Both**

   Sometimes, both the patient as well as the physician may not be prepared to do the skin prick test. Under such circumstances, the blood allergy test would be the most viable option.

4. **Neither**

   There are instances when the patient would want a skin allergy test and the physician is willing to do the test but still blood test would be an ideal option. This is when a component analysis of the allergenic food is required.

Role of Laboratory

A lab testing would be helpful in the following scenarios:

1. Anaphylaxis:

   After a severe allergic reaction without a known cause to identify a trigger.

2. Food Allergy:

- When there are persisting or intermittent symptoms without any other known reason, especially with concurrent atopic symptoms.
- When experiencing allergic symptoms (itch, angioedema, urticaria, wheezing, and gastroesophageal responses) in association with food exposure.
- When one has limited their diet based on perceived adverse reactions to foods/additives.
- 20 per cent of individuals in the population believe they have adverse reactions to foods but not all these reactions are food allergies, as they are not immune-mediated. Hence, these should not

be tested unless they may be needed for patient satisfaction.

3. Urticaria (indication for lab testing):
   - Acute
     - When the reaction has occurred within an hour of ingestion and lasts <24 hours and
     - In all severe cases and where there is a suspicion of allergy.

   - Chronic
     - There is a high chance of false-positive results leading to unnecessary avoidance of food substances. Chronic idiopathic urticaria rarely needs investigation and can usually just be managed with antihistamines.

4. Eczema/Atopic Dermatitis:
   - Although total IgE is high in atopic dermatitis, the disease is not an IgE mediated disease and allergy tests should be avoided unless there is an additional history of immediate hypersensitivity. House dust mite (HDM) tests are almost always positive.

Role of Serum Based In-Vitro Specific Ige Testing in Allergy Diagnosis

The blood test for a specific type of allergen will be helpful in the following way:

1. Identification and quantification of an allergen-specific IgE which can be a food or aeroallergen.
2. Predictive of immunotherapy respondents
   The level of the blood result does not generally predict the possible severity of an allergic reaction, except for some specialist component tests. Patients on immunotherapy may show no change in levels of allergen despite improvement in symptoms.
3. Predictor of tolerance to food allergens in children
   This is one very important aspect of the testing as allergenic food consists of various sub-components.

For example, the different molecular components of peanuts, an important food, have been listed below.

Allergen	**Frequency of Reactivity (per cent)**
Ara h 1	>90
Ara h 2	>90
Ara h 3	44
Ara h 4	44
Ara h 5	16
Ara h 6	38
Ara h 7	44
Ara h 8	85

In the above case, if we know the component of the peanut allergens in the patient's blood, we can safely determine the outcome based on the reactivity of that particular component. As an example, the presence of Ara h 1 in the blood is dangerous because of high reactivity while Ara h 5 presence is safe because of low reactivity in peanut-positive patients.

Also, some components are highly allergenic and heat-stable. Heating and cooking have no impact on these components. There are other components which are labile and not so allergenic. These components can be destroyed by heating or cooking. The presence of these labile components is a predictor of the development of tolerance with time and thus, a good omen.

Testing Methods for Specific IgE

1. **Radio Allegro Sorbent Test (RAST)**
   Allergens are chemical substances. Due to this property, radioactively labelled anti-IgE is added, which attaches to the specific IgE bound to the allergen. The amount of specific IgE can be then estimated from the amount of bound radioactivity. Since at least 2010, health organisations in the US have recommended that the RAST be abandoned as a diagnostic test for allergy in favour of more sensitive fluorescence enzyme-labelled assays (FEIA). The latter method is the most reliable technique to date. It is costly, but no doubt helps in proving or disproving the presence of an allergy.

2. **Fluorescent-Enzyme Immunoassay (FEIA)**
   The latest and best laboratory method to identify aeroallergens is the fluorescent-enzyme

immunoassay (FEIA) method. Although this has not been validated for most of the food allergens, its reliability is the same as the skin prick test for nuts, eggs, milk, seafood, and most cereals. The fluorescent-enzyme immunoassay (FEIA) helps to identify the aeroallergens as well as the food allergens that the patient may have an allergy to. This is a reliable method with a sensitivity towards some allergens being almost the same as that of a skin prick test. However, it is costly and needs a much-detailed history before it is done.

3. **Advance Test**

   Newer tests have been developed in recent times such as the basophil activation test (BAT). The basophil activation tests have a role in the diagnosis and follow-up of food and drug allergies. However, it is not easily available for clinical practice and is currently used only in research settings.

4. **Food Component Analysis—Microtek Assay**

   Food items consist of different components that can broadly be classified as stable or as labile allergens. The stable allergens are generally associated with or can be considered as a predictor of severe systemic reactions, whereas labile allergens are associated with mild to moderate reactions. Cooking food destroys this allergen and the food can be often tolerated. The presence of positivity to the labile allergen is an indicator that in future, the patient will outgrow the allergy to that particular food. A positive stable allergen is an indicator that the patient is less likely to outgrow the allergy.

Hence, when the patient is positive for a particular allergen like peanut or wheat, we need to find whether they are positive for stable or labile allergen components of that food or for both. This can be done by a special test called component-resolved diagnosis (CRD). This is a blood test using microtek assay which specifically lists the different components of the food item and gives their levels in the blood. Based on these values and on our knowledge of which components are stable and which are labile, we can confidently advise the patients about whether they will get anaphylaxis or whether they can safely eat it in the cooked form but most importantly, also concur whether they can outgrow the allergy to that food with time or not.

Case Scenario

A male child, Veer, born from a normal delivery and strictly breastfed, came at the age of 5 years with a history of repeated episodes of vomiting, especially following milk ingestion and a constant nasal congestion. In infancy, he had developed a rash on milk ingestion, so it had been stopped. It was restarted one year back and no rash had developed and there was also no family history of allergies. The people in the family were strict vegetarians and didn't even have eggs. Also, there was a cat in a neighbour's house and cattle were being bred in another immediate neighbour's house. On examination, except for inferior turbinate hypertrophy, there was no significant finding. So, the component analysis was done for 300 allergens and the results were as follows.

Aeroallergens such as pollen, mites, and moulds and those from pigeons, dogs, cats, and cockroaches were negative. The insects and latex influences were also negative. All plant food came out negative. Cos milk Bos d4, 5, and

8 were negative. The child also tested negative for other allergens from cattle milk, eggs, and seafood. The positive results came from cattle meat Bos d 6 (serum albumin), 3.51 goat epithelil, cap epithelia 2.5, and the total IgE was less than 20.

Bos d 6 is a heat-labile allergen found in cow's milk and beef. The degree of cross-reactivity between Bos d 6 and other members of the serum albumin allergen family is usually high. A very high degree of cross-reactivity has been described between Fel d 2 from cats and Sus d 1 from pigs (cat-pork syndrome).

Also, sensitisation to beef was detected. Allergic symptoms associated with beef range from gastrointestinal symptoms to anaphylaxis. Apart from it, there was a major manifestation is exacerbation of underlying eczema. Beef allergy can be caused via sensitisation to serum albumin (Bos d 6), or via sensitisation to alpha-gal, a heat-resistant sugar in non-primate mammals. Clinical reactions to alpha-gal often have a delay of 3-6 hours. Tick bites are the main sensitisation route in such as case.

The final conclusion was that the environment of the child was conducive to the outcome. The highly unhygienic cattle were infested with ticks which probably led to the positivity in spite of never consuming meat in the family.

The above case was presented as a poster at the EAACI (European Academy) conference in Hamburg in 2023.

Salient Points

- Clinical diagnosis, especially a good patient history forms the essence of allergy diagnosis.
- Laboratories are only for supportive and confirmatory tests for the clinical diagnosis.
- Specific allergens should be identified by the FEIA method but unfortunately, it is costly.
- Component-resolved diagnosis is the future in the management of allergies.

2

Skin Prick Test

Skin prick testing is the method of identifying the incriminating agent. This chapter describes the method, precautions, and limitations of skin prick testing, and its use in different conditions. There are many apprehensions about the testing and thus, the need to demystify it.

Introduction

Allergen testing is an important prerequisite for specific allergy treatment. It supports in the identification of infants at increased risk for the development of allergic diseases at a later stage and thereby lays an effective precedent for specific allergy treatment including specific allergen avoidance measures, relevant pharmacotherapy, and specific allergy vaccination.

The cases in which the child needs to be tested include:

- Recurrent possible allergic symptoms
- Need for continuous prophylactic treatment
- Testing for a specific allergen, irrespective of age

Also, the extent of allergy tests will depend on:

- Age of the child
- Positive family history of allergic diseases
- The character of the symptoms

Steps in Allergen Testing

There are two primary steps when it comes to testing an allergen and they are as follows:

1. Taking detailed case history
2. Test to determine IgE sensitisation
    - Skin prick test (SPT) and/or
    - Allergen-specific IgE in serum

There are newer tests available which are primarily used for research purposes or in institutes exclusively. Food allergy can be diagnosed by a SPT, but an oral challenge test is the gold standard.

How Is Skin Testing Done?

Skin testing is done by the widely practised skin prick test (SPT) using a lancet or by the intradermal test using an insulin syringe. The SPT has a high sensitivity, low specificity, greater selection of antigen, is less expensive, and requires minimal equipment. It is also safer and less painful than the intradermal test and unlike with intradermal test, anaphylaxis with SPT is rare.

Steps in Skin Prick Test (SPT)

1. Clean the forearm with spirit or propanol liquid.
2. A drop of different allergens is placed in different circles drawn on the forearm or on the back in the case of young infants.
3. A lancet of steel or sharp plastic is used to prick the epidermis. There should be no bleeding as it can lead to false-positive results.

4. Wait for at least 20 minutes.
5. Wheal formation of more than 3 mm with negative saline control and more than 3 mm histamine control would be suggestive of allergy.

(For more details, check the videos and images on www.allermy.com)

Convincing the Child for a Skin Prick Test

Sometimes, working with a child can be slightly difficult, but this is very obvious and natural considering the age factor and the fears they might have. There are many ways to convince them and among these are:

- Show videos of children of a very small age undergoing a test without any fuss, especially being done by you.
- Try doing at least two tests on the parents or other attendees in order to reassure the child.
- Incorporate a lot of diversionary tactics such as playing their favourite movie on a cell phone, talking about their school or home, or making them recite their favourite poem or any religious mantra which they may have learnt.

Side Effects

World over, there's no reported patient who has had an anaphylactic reaction following a skin prick test. There are a few patients, especially young girls, who would collapse during the procedure and have vomiting too. In such cases, the staff shouldn't panic and take utmost care of the attendees and the child. In such a case, it is advisable to put the patient in a lying position and give them a glass of water.

Interpretation

As mentioned, the clinical relevance of SPT is in the diagnosis of food allergy, asthma, and allergic rhinitis, directing the different treatment options accordingly. But in the case of children, it has a special relevance. For example, a child with positive skin prick test having wheeze and cough without fever and progressive symptoms is more likely to be a persistent wheezer. The allergic child who needs allergy skin prick testing may present any of the following types of allergies:

1. **Food Allergy**

   The skin prick test is a useful procedure for evaluating clinical reactivity, but it is important to understand that:

   - Clinical relevance is only possible in the presence of a consistent association with a history of symptoms on exposure to the concerned allergen.
   - Negative predictive value (>95 per cent) with a negative skin test excludes IgE mediated food allergy. In such a case, we can certainly exclude food allergy and the patient can freely eat the concerned food substance.
   - Positive predictive value is less than 50 per cent. In such a case, a clinical correlation has to be done and if present, then a food challenge should preferably be done.

- History suggestive of food allergy and a positive SPT is supportive.
- Larger SPT wheals correlate with a positive food challenge. If the SPT wheals are greater than 8mm for milk, peanut, and egg, then it has a 95 per cent clinical reactivity.
- Normal subjects may show a reaction to foods consumed on a regular basis. South Indians regularly eat rice only. So, it would be normal for them to be positive on an SPT albeit ≤ 3mm.
- Positive SPT in non-allergic patients predisposes to future allergic disease. If there is no clinical reactivity and the challenge is negative, it means the individual is sensitised.
- SPT will be negative in cases of food intolerance and non-IgE mediated food allergy.

Any food substance that can be pricked with the lancet can be tested using the prick-to-prick method. In this method, we prick the food and then the skin. It is safe, sterile, and more reliable than using food extracts with reagents as extracts of foods can lose much of their reactivity, unlike raw food. Through prick-to-prick tests, we have the liberty to test a wide variety of allergens, unlike the blood test where the available tests are very limited.

2. Anaphylaxis

After anaphylaxis, if the cause is not known, the patient will need to be tested after complete recovery. A minimum gap of six weeks is needed.

3. **Urticaria**
   Indications for skin prick testing include:
   - **Acute**
     In cases where the reaction has occurred within an hour of ingestion and lasts less than 24 hours. It can also be done in all severe cases and where there is a suspicion of allergy.
   - **Chronic**
     Not recommended due to a high chance of false-positive results, leading to unnecessary avoidance of food substances.

4. **Eczema/Atopic Dermatitis**
   In atopic dermatitis, T-cells play a role in 80 per cent of cases. It is an IgE mediated disease. Skin prick test can be done to identify the aeroallergens and food allergens which are aggravating atopic dermatitis.

Case Study

Mrs Shubda, a 40-year-old officer, complained of having developed symptoms of anaphylaxis which required hospitalisation and adrenaline. She developed the symptoms immediately after eating prawns. She was adamant that it was a prawn allergy and wanted it to be tested.

However, after getting a detailed history, I tested her with prawns along with all the ingredients that were used to prepare the prawn dish. The result was:

- Prawn: Negative
- Coriander: Positive

- Red chillies: Positive
- Green chillies: Negative

All of the above were tested, besides other spices. She was advised to take prawns in boiled form and avoid red chillies and coriander.

Salient Points

- Allergen testing begins with taking patient's meticulous history which is followed by a determination of IgE sensitisation.
- The SPT is very safe and more reliable than a blood test.
- Any food item that can be pricked in its natural form can be tested by the prick-to-prick method.
- A negative prick-to-prick test almost rules out the concerned food allergy. For a positive food test, a direct challenge is the gold standard.
- In the management of asthma and allergic rhinitis, a skin prick test is essential to find the aeroallergen for good environmental control.

3
Food Challenges

Oral food challenge is the most reliable method of diagnosis of food allergy. This chapter describes how patients can prepare themselves for an oral challenge and the general method that is followed and the risks involved. It further elaborates types of oral food challenges such as office based and hospital based along with a detailed protocol.

Introduction

Oral food challenges are performed by feeding the patient the suspected food under physician observation. Guidelines from leading world allergy organisations describe oral food challenge (OFC) as the gold standard for diagnosis of IgE mediated and non-IgE mediated food allergy. It is usually conducted to make a diagnosis, to monitor the resolution of a food allergy, and to identify the threshold of responsiveness.

Indications

There are several situations in which physician-supervised oral food challenges are required for diagnosis of food allergic disease.

1. In general, when several foods are under consideration as a cause of symptoms, tests for specific IgE are positive, and the positive predictive

value of a positive SPT for food is only 50 per cent. Hence, it might be necessary to conduct an oral challenge in order to decide about the reintroduction of a food item.

2. If tests for specific IgE are false positive, oral food challenges may be the only way of diagnosis.
3. Oral challenges are also an integral part of a follow-up patients who are likely to lose their clinical reactivity to the food in question. Since a skin test may remain positive for years following the achievement of clinical tolerance to a particular food, oral food challenges are often the only means to determine whether the allergy has been 'outgrown'.

When to Be Done?

OFC can be done for patients of any age with a history of adverse reactions to a food item. OFC can be helpful for:

1. Establishment or exclusion of the diagnosis of food allergy, where the child has been eating regularly earlier but had a recent food reaction.
2. Assessment of tolerance as some food allergies can outgrow with time. Skin prick test and specific IgE are not reliable indicators of tolerance.
3. In clinical trials for scientific purposes.

When Not to Be Done?

OFC can be avoided in the following cases:

1. Where there have been repeated reactions to the particular food.

2. Where there has been a recent episode of anaphylaxis.
3. In some patients, where positive results make the challenges null and void—skin prick test or serum food specific IgE results are above the 95 per cent predictive value for positive reactions—and the concerned food has already shown clinical reactivity.

Factors to Be Considered

1. Patient or family preference of the food to be challenged. And if the test comes out negative, their interest in incorporating the food item into their daily diet.
2. Risk of an allergic reaction and the impact of a positive challenge on the patient and the family (in paediatric patients).
3. Nutritional importance of the food being avoided, especially in the case of milk.

Key Points to Keep in Mind

There are a few important points to keep in mind before the oral food challenge is planned:

1. Oral food challenges to baked milk and baked eggs have been implemented clinically in varied ways, with some physicians aiming to demonstrate tolerance to full servings and others intending to put a small amount in the diet.
2. The protocol and clinical assessment of symptoms or signs of a positive reaction during an oral food challenge is influenced by age.

3. The oral food challenge procedure is tailored to the type of expected reaction (immediate, delayed, and cofactors [e.g., nonsteroidal anti-inflammatories, exercise, etc.]).
4. Avoid all suspected food allergens confirmed at diagnosis.
5. Caution with inadvertent ingredients since these too can cause reactions.
6. When there is a list of foods the family wants to introduce, it is advisable to avoid their introduction all at once.

Types of Food Challenges

Given below are the various types of food challenges.

1. **Double-Blind**
   Both patients and doctors are unaware of the type or content of food being given.

2. **Single-Blind**
   The doctor is aware of the food being given but the patient is totally unaware of it.

3. **Open**
   Both doctor and patient are aware of the content of food. This is the easiest and most common. However, false positives can happen in this case.

4. **Double-Blind Placebo Controlled (DBPCFC)**
   The doctor and patient are unaware of the type of food given. In addition, the patient is also given a placebo with no one knowing which is food and which is the placebo. This is the gold standard but very cumbersome to conduct.

5. **Exercise + Oral Challenge**
   The patient is given a small portion of the food and then made to exercise half an hour later on the treadmill for 20 to 25 minutes and monitored for changes in clinical condition.

Note: Double-blind challenge is the procedure that's generally recommended, especially if a positive challenge outcome is expected.

Procedure for Oral Food Challenge

1. Suspected food allergens should be eliminated for 1 to 2 weeks prior to the food challenge.
2. Antihistamines should be stopped for the appropriate period of time to promote a normal histamine response.
3. On the day of admission:
   - The patient should be without symptoms and should be fasting.
   - Food intended for challenge should be started with minimal doses and increased at regular intervals (15-30 minutes).
   - The quantity of the last challenge should be related to the age of the patient (meal-sized portion).
4. Challenge with different foods should be planned on different days.
5. Oral food challenges for high-risk patients are best performed by immunologists and specialists experienced in treating food allergies.
6. Challenges should be carried out in clinical settings equipped with resuscitation facilities and staffed

with trained allied health personnel, especially in the cases of children who have had a previous reaction to the food or are positive on testing.

Case Scenario

Aanya, a 15-year-old child, believed to have vague egg and nut allergy, had been avoiding these foods since childhood. She is due to go to a hostel soon and keen to have eggs again in her diet.

In this case, we proceeded with SPT for egg, peanut, cashew, and almonds, which were all negative. As egg was one of the foods she was keen to eat again, we proceeded to an oral food challenge and she tolerated the consumption of eggs, post which she has been eating eggs at least 2-3 times in her diet.

Salient Points

- OFC is needed to either confirm or rule out food allergy when diagnosis is in doubt.
- OFC can help prevent unnecessary food restrictions.
- Primary types of food challenges include open, single-blind, double-blind, and placebo-controlled.

4

Oral Home Challenge

Home challenge can be a daunting undertaking for the parents but in special circumstances, it may be required to be done. Also, one should know the exact method of conducting it as it is very important.

The Need for Oral Home Challenge for Children

Most children who previously had developed an allergic reaction to milk will outgrow their milk allergy in later stages. The sooner dairy products are reintroduced into your child's diet, the sooner their life will return to normal and concerns about future reactions can be allayed. Avoiding milk products unnecessarily can make the allergy worse and also make it more difficult for your child to grow out of it later.

It has also been shown that many children who react to fresh milk, cheese, and yoghurt can tolerate milk in a cooked or baked form. Cooking or baking milk, especially when mixed with flour and other foods, makes the milk less likely to cause allergic reactions. Thus, it is important to introduce cooked and processed milk into your child's diet. This will help to make your child's diet less restrictive and more interesting and enjoyable. It may also help your child to improve their tolerance to cow's milk and dairy products.

But exactly when your child should try milk products should be discussed with a healthcare professional. The timing will depend on what type of dairy product your child reacted to previously and the reaction they had. In general, dairy products should be tried again if your child has not had any reactions over the last six months.

Pre-Challenge Checklist

Some important things to keep in mind before the challenge are as follows:

1. Ensure your child is well. If your child has had a flare of their eczema, asthma, or hay fever, or has taken antihistamines in the last five days, do not undertake the challenge.
2. Do not attempt the challenge at home if your child has ever had any breathing problems or has fainted or shown floppiness after having milk.
3. Seek medical advice.
4. Have a supply of antihistamines available, for example cetirizine, in case a reaction occurs.
5. Pick a day when you will be able to observe your child for at least four hours. Always avoid public holidays.

Steps in Oral Challenge

The steps involved in an oral challenge are as follows:

1. Give the child a drop of milk or an equivalent dairy product recommended by your doctor or dietitian. You can also dip a clean finger in milk, shake off the excess, and then touch your child's tongue with the finger.

2. Wait 15 minutes. If no reaction occurs, then continue.
3. Give your child ¼ of a teaspoon (1¼ ml) of milk. Wait 15 minutes and if no reaction occurs, continue.
4. Give your child half a teaspoon (2½ ml) of milk. Wait 15 minutes and if no reaction occurs, continue.
5. Give your child a teaspoon (5 ml) of milk. Wait 15 minutes and if no reaction occurs, continue.
6. Double this amount every 15 minutes if no reaction occurs, until a cup (200 ml) of milk has been taken, provided this does not exceed their normal intake volume.

When to Stop the Challenge

If any of the following reactions/symptoms develop, then the challenge should be stopped immediately.

- Red, raised, or itchy rash.
- Swelling where the food has been applied.
- Vomiting, tummy pain, loose stools, etc.
- Difficulty in breathing or noisy breathing.
- Wheeze or persistent cough.
- Dizziness, feeling faint, floppiness, etc.

Note: If a rash or swelling develops give your child an antihistamine and the symptoms should resolve within half an hour. In the unlikely event of breathing problems or faintness, call for help. You can dial 108 or take your child to the nearest accident and emergency department.

Also, in such a case, do not conduct another challenge and instead, seek medical advice.

Post-Challenge Analysis

The two scenarios post challenge are as follows:

1. If no reaction occurs over the next two hours, you can introduce milk back into your child's diet.
2. If a reaction does occur, continue with a dairy-free diet, and try challenging with milk again in 4-6 months' time.

Points to Remember

Some children are often fearful (as are their parents) of taking foods that have previously caused a reaction. If your child is old enough, try to explain why the challenge is being done and its significance. Some challenges may only get part way through, and a reaction might occur. If this happens and if there are no breathing problems or faintness, talk to your healthcare professional and try reintroducing the food again in 4 to 6 months. An important thing to keep in mind is that any food that previously had caused anaphylaxis should never be challenged at home.

Milk Ladder (As Per NWHA of NHS UK Guidelines)

Given below are two milk ladder tables specifying the types of food and quantity details when reintroducing milk. This milk ladder can be used for children who have previously suffered from delayed skin or gastrointestinal reactions, as well as in children who have had hives or skin swellings.

Table 1: Milk Ladder (Which Foods)

Stage	Foods
1.	**Biscuits containing milk** • Malted milk biscuit • Shortcake **Note**: Most digestive biscuits no longer contain milk.
2.	**Baked products** • Plain cakes or plain muffins • Scones • Milk loaf • Croissants • Brioche
3.	**Baked products cooked for less time** • Scotch pancakes • Cheese powder flavourings, quavers, and wotsits
4.	**Foods containing cheese or milk** • Cream or cheese on toast, macaroni cheese, pizza, lasagna, pasta bake, etc. • Chocolate • Shepherd's pie/mash with butter and milk in sauces • Soups or meals/purees containing milk rice pudding/custards

contd ...

Stage	Foods
5.	**Less processed milk** • Yoghurt • Fromage frais • Soft cheese • Butter
5.	**Less processed milk** • Yoghurt • Fromage frais • Soft cheese • Butter

Table 2: Milk Ladder (How Much Food)

Stage	Amount of Food
1.	Grain of rice size (400mg)
2.	Pea size (1000mg/1g)
3.	Teaspoon size (5g)
4.	Tablespoon size (15g)
5.	¼ portion
6.	½ standard portion
7.	Full standard portion

Note: Give the food at least 3 times a week once tolerated. Increase each stage weekly if possible.

Points to Remember

- Do not attempt the reintroduction of dairy products at home if your child has previously suffered from breathing problems or floppiness after drinking milk or other dairy products.
- Do not increase food portions or introduce new foods when your child is unwell.
- Start at the step as per the advice of your doctor or dietitian. Your child may already be tolerating some foods from the ladder, so you can then progress from there.
- In case any issue arises, do not stop completely; go back to the previously tolerated stage until further review by your health professional. Wheat free and egg free options of the milk ladder are available and should be discussed with your dedicated health professional.

Case Scenario

Arnav, a 7-year-old boy, had not taken milk for years as he had reacted adversely to cow's milk as a toddler. The reaction was in the form of a rash around the mouth. There was no respiratory difficulty nor any gastrointestinal symptoms. His blood work for the different milk was as follows: Cow milk casein 0.38, sheep milk 0.35, camel and mare's milk < 0.10, and goat milk < 0.10.

We first gave him, in graded doses, camel milk as he was negative. Since he showed no reaction, we introduced cow milk products starting with biscuits followed by milk bread then curd and lastly, cheese. Since he showed no adverse reaction to all of them, we started him on boiled cow's milk in a graded way at home. It was done on a Monday in the morning hours, and we were informed about it at every hour. After tolerating a full dose, he was put on regular cow milk.

Salient Points

- Always start with a product in a cooked form.
- The cooked or boiled form is preferred, and it should strictly be in graded quantity.

Section IV
MANAGEMENT

1

Treatment

The definitive treatment of food allergy is as brief as this chapter alone.

Introduction

'Na rahega baans, na bajegi bansuri' is an Indian proverb which literally means when there is no flute, there wouldn't be any tune from it. It implies that in the absence of the cause of the problem, there would not be any problems. Simply put, the treatment of food allergy comprises correctly identifying the food causing the problem and eliminating it completely from the diet.

Oral Second-Generation Antihistamine Doses

The drugs which are given when the symptoms occur are mainly anti-allergic consisting of 2nd generation antihistamines. The dosages to be used are mentioned in the table on the next page.

The other drugs that may be added are oral steroids, antiemetics for vomiting, and H2 blockers for acidity. All drugs that are given will only overcome the symptoms once the food allergen has started the cascade of the allergic reaction including anaphylaxis.

A new modality of treatment in research and practise worth mentioning is immunotherapy, which is now commercially available exclusively for peanut allergy.

Drug	Age-Wise Dosing	Conditions Requiring Dose Adjustment	Clinically Relevant Drug-Drug Interactions
Cetirizine	6 months to < 2 years: 6 to 23 months: 2.5mg OD 12 to 23 months: 2.5mg OD or BD 2 to 5 years: 2.5mg OD/BD or 5 mg OD 6 to 11 years: 5 or 10 mg OD >12 years: 5mg or 10mg OD	Renal and hepatic impairment	Unlikely
Levocetirizine	6 months to 5 years: 1.25mg OD 6 to 11 years: 2.5mg OD >12 years: 5mg OD	Renal and hepatic impairment	Unlikely
Fexofenadine	2 to 12 years: 30mg BD >12 years: 120 or 180 mg OD	Renal impairment	Unlikely
Loratadine	1 to 2 years: 2.5mg OD 2 to 12 years: 5mg or 10mg OD >12 years: 10mg OD	Hepatic impairment	Unlikely
Desloratadine	6 to 11months: 1 mg OD 12 months to 5 years: 1.25mg OD 6 to 11 years: 2.5mg OD >12 years: 5 mg OD	Renal and hepatic impairment	Unlikely
Bilastine	>12 years: 20 mg 6 to 12 years: 10 mg Below 6 years: Not recommended	Nil	Unlikely

Credits @ 2022 Indian Academy of Paediatrics

Mechanism of Immunotherapy

In specific immunotherapy (SIT), we gradually expose the patient to small amounts of allergen in order to induce tolerance. It modifies the course of allergic disease in children and adults suffering from peanut allergy. It is also very widely used in cases of rhinitis, conjunctivitis, and asthma. SIT halts the atopic march and prevents the development of asthma in a patient with rhinitis and vice versa. It also prevents the development of new allergies in an individual who already has allergies. Specific immunotherapy is the only real possible disease-modifying treatment for allergic patients. It is available as an oral tablet, and the period of treatment is three to five years, and at the moment, it is recommended for milk and peanut allergy only.

Case Scenario

Jabeen, an 8-year-old NRI, born and brought up in Australia, was suffering from multiple allergies since infancy. She did not have allergic rhinitis or asthma but had atopic dermatitis which was aggravated by foods. The concerning food was peanut that had caused, on multiple occasions, at least 3 times a reaction in the form of urticaria and lip swelling. At the age of 5 years, she had an attack of anaphylaxis and required an EpiPen. Her parents started her on oral peanut immunotherapy at the age of 6 years. For the last one and half years, she has been taking peanut oral immunotherapy and has never had any episode of urticaria in spite of an occasion of accidental ingestion of peanuts in a marinated chicken 16 months after the start of therapy.

Salient Points

- Complete avoidance is the only definite treatment.
- All other treatment is symptomatic.
- Immunotherapy is in its nascent stage but has a future.

2
Prevention

Once a person is diagnosed as food allergic with the possibility of anaphylaxis, it can be a terrifying shock. However, all this can be well managed by prudent and preventative measures at every stage of their life.

Introduction

An important aspect of managing food allergies effectively is education and awareness. Thus, it is not only important to educate the patient with an allergy, but also other students, caregivers, parents, and even the general public, by and large, about the triggers of an allergic reaction and the management plan.

- Younger children are dependent on their parents and caregivers when it comes to managing allergies but as they grow older, they can be educated on how to handle their allergies. Parents should take the initiative to explain the seriousness of a possible food allergic reaction when they are mature enough to understand.
- Individuals with food allergies should be able to describe their allergies, enquire about possible triggers in the food they eat, and not accept food randomly from others.

- Caregivers, including school staff, should have optimised strategies to effectively manage an allergic reaction. They should also be given age-appropriate education about food allergies and policies about bullying and dealing with nutritional aspects of food allergy in children.
- The general public should be educated about the serious nature of an allergic reaction.

Community Education

When it comes to managing food allergies, the role of community education can't be overstated. Some steps that can be taken to better tackle food allergies outside hospitals and in schools/colleges are as follows:

1. Have the latest medical information and detailed plan of care from a healthcare professional.
2. Education of the staff and peers in recognition and management of allergic reactions.
3. Patient education about the management of allergic reactions.
4. Public awareness campaigns on food allergies and their management.

Managing Food Allergy and Anaphylaxis Outside the Home (Children)

For children having severe food allergies, there are some important protocols to keep in mind. Firstly, details of the child's allergic triggers must be included in the documents upon admission into the school. Also, a detailed anaphylaxis action plan, certified by a doctor, must be submitted to the school. It must carry details such as:

1. Important details pertaining to the child along with a photo and if possible, also include parents and the treating doctor's details.
2. Clear mention of the identified allergenic triggers, description of allergy symptoms—mild/moderate and severe symptoms—and treatment prescribed, including details for auto-injector use.
3. Anaphylaxis action plans must be updated periodically with changes in medications and auto-injectors, ideally every 12 months.
4. For those with concurrent asthma and food allergies, asthma treatment must be optimised.
5. Pre-school/school management must work in close conjunction with parents of children with food allergies, to devise strategies for minimising risk for exposure to potential allergens and have a healthcare plan for accidental exposure.

Also, as mentioned before, the education of the staff in the recognition and management of an allergic reaction is of vital importance. This should cover a few basic aspects like types of allergic reactions, common causes of food allergy, and symptoms and signs of mild/moderate and severe allergic reactions, including anaphylaxis. It is also important to educate them about the first-aid management plan and medications for emergency use, including epinephrine auto-injectors, with practical sessions. All these aspects should be reinforced and checked periodically.

Given below are certain ground rules that need to be followed when encountering a possible allergic reaction:

1. The emergency action plan must be followed as *given by the child's medical practitioner.*
2. Make the child lie flat without allowing them to sit or stand. If in the lying position, the child finds it difficult to breathe, then make the patient sit.
3. Call for help and remove the possible allergy-causing substance from the individual's vicinity.
4. If in doubt of a severe allergic reaction or anaphylaxis, always first administer the epinephrine auto-injector and then other medications can be given.
5. Antihistamines and corticosteroids are not the first line of medications in a severe allergic reaction.
6. The individual needs to be taken to the nearest medical facility for further observation, even after giving the epinephrine auto-injector.
7. The staff must be trained to administer the epinephrine auto-injector as the child/adult having an allergic reaction may be unwell to do so themselves.
8. Emphasis must be given to the fact that allergic reactions are unexpected, and many a time, they can be severe and occur at an unexpected place (outside of home).
9. Epinephrine auto-injectors must be replaced upon expiry.

How to Reduce the Risk of an Allergen Exposure

Some of the ways we can reduce the risk of an allergen exposure are as follows:

1. Ideally, the food must be packed and carried from home.
2. Food sharing with friends must be discouraged.
3. Labelling of all food containers and bottles to be followed to minimise accidental exposure to food triggers.
4. Food should not be given to children with a food allergy without parental engagement and permission. For example, at birthday parties, primary school, childcare places, etc.
5. When planning for out-of-school activities such as excursions, school outings, and camps, it is important to take into consideration the catering requirements of the food-allergic child and also the emergency plan, including access to emergency medication and medical care.
6. Art activities must have articles devoid of possible food allergens.
7. Encourage older children and adults to cultivate a habit of reading food labels.

Managing Food Allergies in Higher-Grade Children

In primary school and high school, food restrictions or bans are not useful risk minimisation strategies. In fact, teenagers and young adults (with food allergies) in this age group are at a higher risk of fatal anaphylaxis. While issues surrounding food allergen avoidance are applicable to all age groups, as children approach their teenage years, education regarding self-management, outings (where there is a higher probability of exposure to unlabeled food), and alcohol exposure (which can lead to reduced vigilance) is important.

Case Scenario

A 10-year-old girl, with a background history of asthma, was brought to the casualty at the hospital. For the past two days, she had been suffering from cough and wheezing and showed symptoms of a mild upper respiratory tract infection which could have been due to the ongoing flu season. Also, at the time, the patient had been using a Levosalbutamol inhaler more than she had done in the past, but with no improvement in her symptoms. On that particular day, she was having difficulty breathing and her lips and tongue had turned blue. In casualty, her oxygen saturation came out to be 90 per cent with respiratory rate being 38 cycles per minute. She had chest retractions and wheezing on auscultation. She was treated with salbutamol and ipratropium/oxygen nebulisation along with parental steroids and other medications. On probing, it was found that she had a history of good control of her asthma with good medication compliance and no exercise and night-induced symptoms. She also had a history of wheezing and hives on exposure to peanuts and eggs for which she was prescribed an injectable epinephrine and an antihistamine for any accidental exposure. She also told us that she had been severely bullied by her friends, mainly because of her food allergies.

Examinations revealed that she had eaten traces of peanut chikki which was put in her lunch box by one of her classmates. This led to her having anxiety issues about going to school. The case emphasises the importance of close monitoring of children, especially when outside the house.

Salient Points

- Education of the staff and peers in the recognition and management of allergic reactions is paramount.
- Create public awareness campaigns on food allergies and their management.

Section V

SPECIFIC FOOD TRIGGERS AND ADDITIVES

1
Diagnosis of Common Food Allergens

Among the numerous food allergies, the most commonly seen are milk, egg, wheat, latex, peanut, tree nuts, sesame, and seafood allergy. Milk allergy has been dealt with in a previous chapter. This chapter provides a practical approach to the above-mentioned food allergens. This information has been taken and reprinted with permission from the North-Western Health Authority of NHS, UK. However, we have made minor changes in terms of logistics applicable to India.

1. Egg Allergy

- **How common is egg allergy?**

Egg allergy is one of the most common allergies, affecting 1 in 50 children in the UK. It is caused by proteins present in both the egg white and yolk. 80 per cent of children who are allergic to scrambled or boiled eggs can tolerate baked eggs in biscuits and cakes. In this case, your child should continue to eat the baked egg to maintain and improve their tolerance.

- **What are the symptoms of egg allergy?**

Symptoms usually occur immediately after eating the egg. They often consist of a rash (hives or 'nettle' rash), swelling of the lips or around the eyes, and itching. Some children develop an itchy throat, while in some cases, they feel sick, vomit, or have diarrhoea. Severe reactions (anaphylaxis) are much less common but other reactions such as difficulty in breathing (with wheeze or swelling of the mouth or throat) and feeling faint or dizzy can occur. These need urgent medical attention. Delayed reactions may lead to flares of a child's eczema, tummy pain, vomiting, or diarrhoea.

- **How serious is egg allergy?**

Most children only have mild reactions. Severe reactions are uncommon but need urgent medical attention if they occur.

- **How do we diagnose egg allergy?**

Diagnosis is usually based on a history of a typical reaction. Allergy tests such as skin prick tests and blood tests provide evidence of reactions to raw eggs. They can be positive in patients who are fine with cooked eggs. Where the history is unclear or we want to know if the child has outgrown their egg allergy, an oral challenge is required.

- **How to avoid eggs?**

Cooking and baking make eggs less likely to cause an allergic reaction. Although a child may get hives or swelling if they touch raw eggs in cake mix, they can usually tolerate the mix once it has been baked into cakes or biscuits. If the biscuits and cakes can be tolerated, these foods should not be taken out of their diet, as they hel the child grow out of their egg allergy more quickly. In children who have had severe reactions, all egg-containing foods listed below might need to be avoided.

Egg white	**Egg yolk**	**Egg solids/powder**
Ovalbumin	Livetin	Ovoglobulin
Ovomucin	Egg albumin	Egg lecithin (E322)
Ovo-vitellin		

Lecithin can be made from egg, soya, or sunflower. If the type of lecithin used is not specified, check with the manufacturer. It is important to read all food labels and packaging before consumption.

- **Can vaccinations be given to a child with an egg allergy?**

Mumps, measles, and rubella (MMR) vaccine can be given to all children with egg allergy. No special precautions are required. Eight hundred UK children with egg allergy, a third of whom had previously suffered anaphylactic reactions to eggs, were given the flu vaccine in the 'Sniffle study' and none suffered a serious allergic reaction. The flu vaccine can be given to anyone with an egg allergy but with caution.

- **What can I do if my child has a reaction?**

The child should be provided with details regarding what to do if they have another reaction. This plan is usually termed as 'allergy management plan'. This plan can be divided into two broad categories:

1. Mild reactions which include hives, swelling, or vomiting, but no breathing problems or faintness. In such a scenario, get the child to spit out the food, if possible. Also, the child should be given an antihistamine.
2. Severe reactions which include difficulty in breathing (wheezing, noisy breathing, blue colour, etc.), swelling in the throat (noisy breathing and drooling), feeling faint or dizzy, and looking very pale. In such a scenario, lay the child down with their legs raised and get help straight away and dial 108, stating the cause as anaphylaxis (ana-fil-ak-sis). If you have an adrenaline pen, use it.

Note: If your child has suffered breathing problems or faintness, eggs may first be tried in a hospital setting.

- **Who needs to know about my child's egg allergy?**

It is important to inform the nursery/school and any after-school clubs. Any other child carers and helpers will also need to know.

- **Can my child grow out of their egg allergy?**

Half of children will grow out of their allergy to eggs by 5 years of age, particularly if they are able to consume baked egg products.

***

2. Wheat Allergy

- **How common is wheat allergy?**

3-5 children in every 1,000 in Europe have an allergy to wheat. It is seen most commonly in infants and preschool children.

- **What are the symptoms of wheat allergy?**

Immediate reactions occur within minutes of exposure and include an itchy rash (hives), swelling, vomiting, diarrhoea, runny nose, and itchy eyes. Severe reactions are much less common but can include difficulty in breathing (with wheeze or swelling in the throat) and feeling faint or dizzy. Some people develop symptoms with wheat only after vigorous exercise (exercise-induced wheat-associated allergy).

Also, delayed reactions occur several hours after eating the food and the symptoms include tummy pain, vomiting, diarrhoea, and worsening of eczema. Coeliac disease or gluten intolerance is a delayed reaction to wheat. People with coeliac disease do not get hives or breathing issues but can have belly aches, diarrhoea, or generally, a run-down feeling.

- **How serious is wheat allergy?**

Most people with wheat allergy only have mild reactions. Severe reactions affecting the child's breathing can occur, particularly in those with bad asthma and these need urgent medical attention when there is a reaction.

- **How to avoid wheat?**

It is important to read the ingredient list carefully. Products like breaded cheese, sausages, beef burgers, Quorn (used as meat substitute), gravy granules, stock cubes, soya sauces, and beverages (malted milk, Ovaltine) can contain wheat. Sometimes, a label may not specify wheat but another form of wheat like bran, semolina, couscous, rusk, or flour. Oil that has been used to fry food containing wheat like fish fingers can lead to a reaction.

People allergic to wheat need to be aware of the risk of cross-contamination in restaurants, bakeries, and loosely sold products. Most children can tolerate corn, rice, oats, barley, buckwheat, tapioca, sago, and quinoa. Also, advice should be sought from a dietitian in case of any doubts or queries.

- **How do we diagnose wheat allergy?**

The diagnosis of wheat allergy is based on the history of a typical reaction after contact with wheat. Positive allergy tests (skin prick or blood IgE) support the diagnosis where symptoms come on immediately or with exercise, but should not be used alone, as people can have positive allergy tests but tolerate wheat without getting a reaction.

Skin prick tests are safe and can be done in the clinic, provided that the child has not had any antihistamines for a few days. Blood tests are not affected by antihistamines. If the diagnosis is uncertain, an oral wheat challenge is sometimes recommended. Coeliac disease is screened for using a special blood test and usually needs a camera test (upper endoscopy) to confirm the diagnosis. These patients are looked after by gastroenterology doctors.

- **Does delaying the introduction of solid food to babies help prevent wheat allergy?**

It is advisable to wean babies to solid food at 4-6 months of age. There is no scientific evidence to suggest that delaying giving wheat to babies any later than this age will protect them from this allergy.

- **How should you manage a reaction?**

After a reaction to wheat, your child should be provided with advice about what to do if they have another reaction. This plan is usually termed as 'allergy management plan'. This plan can be divided into two broad categories:

1. Mild reactions which include hives, swelling, or vomiting, but no breathing problems or faintness. In such a scenario, get the child to spit out the food, if possible. Also, the child should be given an antihistamine.
2. Severe reactions which include difficulty in breathing (wheezing, noisy breathing, blue colour, etc.), swelling in the throat (noisy breathing, drooling), feeling faint or dizzy, and looking very pale. In such a scenario, lay the child down with their legs raised and get help straight away and dial 108, stating the cause as anaphylaxis (ana-fil-ak-sis). If you have an adrenaline pen, use it.

- **Who needs to know about this allergy?**

It is important to inform the nursery/school and any after-school clubs. Any other child carers and helpers will also need to know.

- **Is wheat allergy a lifelong condition?**

Coeliac disease is lifelong, and therefore, patients must continue to avoid all foods containing wheat. About 70 per cent of children will outgrow the other forms of wheat allergy by 6 years of age. If there has been no reaction for a long time, then an oral challenge may be suggested.

- **Is there a cure for wheat allergy?**

Some patients (not those with coeliac disease) can tolerate a little wheat, in which case, they may outgrow their allergy more quickly. Advice should always be sought from your doctor or dietitian before trying to introduce wheat in any form back into your child's diet.

***

3. Soyabean Allergy

- **How common is soya allergy?**

Soy allergy is a reaction to the proteins found in soybeans. Soyabean is a member of the bean family native to East Asia. In the UK, it is seen most frequently in infants and preschool children, with about 4 in 1000 children thought to have the allergy.

- **What are the symptoms of soya allergy?**

About half of children with soy allergy have symptoms that begin immediately after eating food containing soya. Most symptoms are mild and may include a rash (hives or 'nettle' rash), swelling of the lips or around the eyes, and itch. Some children develop an itchy throat, while in some cases, they feel sick, vomit, or have diarrhoea.

Severe reactions are much less common but can include difficulty in breathing (with wheeze or swelling that blocks the mouth or throat) and feeling faint or dizzy (anaphylaxis). Sometimes, symptoms are delayed and occur at a later stage. Common complaints are flares in the child's eczema, colic, and belly ache.

- **How serious is soya allergy?**

Most children with soya allergy only have mild reactions. Severe reactions affecting the child's breathing can occur, particularly in those with bad asthma and these need urgent medical attention.

- **How about other foods?**

One in ten children with a milk allergy is also allergic to soya. This may become apparent when soya milk is tried as an alternative, following the child's reaction to dairy products. Other legumes such as beans, pulses, lentils, and chickpeas can usually be tolerated. If you have any concerns, discuss them with your doctor or dietitian.

- **How do we diagnose soya allergy?**

The diagnosis of soya allergy is based on the history of a typical reaction after contact with soya. Positive skin prick or blood IgE tests can support the diagnosis, but should not be used alone, as many people can have a positive allergy test but may tolerate soya without getting a reaction. Skin prick tests are safe and can be done in a clinic, provided that the child has not had any antihistamines for a few days. Blood tests are not affected by antihistamines. If the diagnosis is uncertain, an oral soya challenge is recommended.

- **How can my child avoid soya?**

Soya is a popular vegetarian alternative to meat and many processed foods contain soya. It is also an ingredient in lots of cow milk and lactose-free recipes. Therefore, it is important to read the ingredients first on pre-packaged foods.

Soya can be avoided by looking for words like soy, miso, tempeh, tofu, bean curd, and hydrolysed or textured vegetable protein. Some Chinese recipes contain soy sprouts and soya sauce and should be avoided. Soya can be found in many readymade meals like pot noodles and tinned spaghetti. It is present in crisps like Quavers and Monster Munch and in most bread available in supermarkets. Also, lecithin, a common food additive, can be processed from soya.

- **How should you manage a reaction?**

After a reaction to soya, your child should be provided with advice about what to do if they have another reaction. This plan is usually termed as 'allergy management plan'. This plan can be divided into two broad categories:

1. Mild reactions which include hives, swelling, or vomiting, but no breathing problems or faintness. In such a scenario, get the child to spit out the food, if possible. Also, the child should be given an antihistamine.
2. Severe reactions which include difficulty in breathing (wheezing, noisy breathing, blue colour, etc.), swelling in the throat (noisy breathing, drooling), feeling faint or dizzy, and looking very pale. In such a scenario, lay the child down with their legs raised and get help straight away and dial 108, stating the cause as anaphylaxis (ana-fil-ak-sis). If you have an adrenaline pen, use it.

- **Who needs to know about this allergy?**

It is important to inform the nursery/school and any after-school clubs. Any other child carers and helpers will also need to know.

- **Is soya allergy a lifelong condition?**

Half of children with soya allergy will outgrow it by 7 years of age. Nearly 70 per cent of children outgrow it by 10 years of age. If there has not been a reaction for a long time, an oral challenge may be suggested.

***

4. Peanut Allergy

- **How common is peanut allergy?**

Peanut allergy consists of a reaction to touching or eating peanut protein (not oil). Peanut allergy is common, affecting 1 in 80 people, or about a million people in the UK.

- **What are the symptoms of peanut allergy?**

Symptoms usually occur immediately after eating the food, although they can occur up to one hour later. They may include a rash ('nettle' rash) or swelling, especially of the face. Some children have an itchy throat, while in some cases, they vomit. Severe reactions (anaphylaxis) are uncommon but can include reactions such as difficulty in breathing (wheezing and noisy breathing), swelling in the throat (noisy breathing, drooling), feeling faint or dizzy, and looking very pale. In such a scenario, lay the child down with their legs raised and get help straight away and dial 108, stating the cause as anaphylaxis (ana-fil-ak-sis).

- **How serious is peanut allergy?**

Severe reactions affecting the child's breathing are uncommon but are more frequent in those with poorly controlled asthma, and these children need urgent medical attention in case of a reaction.

- **Are there likely to be any other food allergies?**

Peanut allergy is more common in children with severe eczema and egg allergy. Children may be allergic only to peanuts or can also be allergic to tree nuts such as cashews and hazelnuts, seeds such as sesame, and legumes such as lentils and peas. Seek medical advice before excluding any of these foods as it may not be necessary.

- **How do we diagnose peanut allergy?**

The diagnosis is suggested by a history of a typical reaction after contact with peanuts. A positive skin prick test or blood allergy antibody (Ige) test can support the diagnosis.

In the absence of a previous allergic reaction to peanuts, allergy tests should not be performed as they can be false positives in many patients, leading to an incorrect diagnosis and unnecessary dietary and lifestyle restrictions.

Skin prick tests are safe and can be done in a clinic, provided that the child has not had any antihistamines for the previous 5 days. Blood tests are not affected by antihistamines. Where there is doubt about the diagnosis, particularly in infants and young preschool children, an oral peanut challenge in a hospital should be considered for accurate diagnosis and to prevent unnecessary dietary and lifestyle restrictions.

- **How to avoid peanuts?**

Avoid eating and touching nuts if you are allergic. Always check the ingredient list on food packets and if in doubt, ask the cook about the recipe. Other names for peanuts are ground nuts and monkey nuts. Also, curries, Indian food, Chinese food, Thai dishes, and pesto sauce can all contain peanuts.

In the UK and EU, packaging regulations require an accurate ingredient list. If peanuts are not listed in the ingredients section and the packaging just states 'may contain traces of nuts', then those food items can be safely eaten. Outside the EU, regulations are different. Be careful when on holiday as foods may be unfamiliar and the ingredients list may not be in English.

- **What about the patient's siblings?**

Siblings of children with peanut allergy should be encouraged to start eating peanut butter early, as delaying the introduction can lead to the development of food allergies. Another point to keep in mind is that they should not share their food with their allergic brother or sister.

- **How should you manage a reaction?**

In the case of peanut allergy, A written management plan will be provided by the doctor and the appropriate medication prescribed should always be available. If a peanut is accidentally eaten, spit the food out straight away and give an antihistamine as soon as possible.

- **Who needs to know about this allergy?**

It is important to inform the nursery/school and any after-school clubs. Any other child carers and helpers will also need to know. Grandparents, relatives, and school friends' parents will also need to know.

- **Is peanut allergy a lifelong condition?**

Most school-age children and adults with peanut allergy will not outgrow the problem and will need to avoid this food throughout their life. In contrast, infants and preschool children can often tolerate some peanut butter and are less likely to suffer from anaphylaxis. It is particularly important to make a correct diagnosis in this group. Your allergy team may suggest a peanut oral challenge in a hospital, possibly allowing a regular reintroduction of peanuts into their diet.

- **Is there a cure for peanut allergy?**

There is no permanent cure for peanut allergy. Allergy centres may offer programs to help preschool children tolerate peanuts, but it is unclear if this can cure the problem. (Refer to the chapter 'Treatment' for more details)

***

5. Tree Nuts Allergy

- **How common is tree nut allergy?**

Tree nut allergy is more common in older children and adults than in infants.

- **What are the symptoms of tree nut allergy?**

Symptoms usually occur straight after eating the nut and the reactions include a rash (hives or 'nettle' rash), swelling of the lips and around the eyes, and itch. In some cases, children get an itchy throat, while in some, they feel sick and vomit. Severe reactions are much less common but can include difficulty in breathing (wheeze or throat swelling) and feeling faint or dizzy. These are features of anaphylaxis and need urgent medical attention.

- **How serious is tree nut allergy?**

Most people with tree nut allergy only have mild reactions. Severe reactions affecting breathing can occur, particularly in those with bad asthma, and these need urgent medical attention.

- **Will my child be allergic to nuts other than the one causing the reaction?**

Some nuts are from the same family and may also cause reactions (this is known as cross-reactivity). Therefore, cross-reacting nuts should be avoided. Examples include cashew and pistachio nuts, and pecan and walnuts. Children with nut allergy should never eat nuts from a mixed nut collection.

It is often easier to avoid all nuts in childhood to avoid confusion for other family members, friends, and school staff. As children grow older and become more independent, they may want to know exactly which nuts they can and cannot eat. This needs to be discussed with your allergist who may repeat allergy tests. Chestnuts, coconut, and seeds like pine nuts, sesame, and sunflower seeds can usually be eaten. Your specialist can advise on the matter.

- **How do we diagnose tree nut allergy?**

The diagnosis of tree nut allergy is based on the history of a typical reaction after contact. Positive skin prick or blood IgE tests can support the diagnosis. Where there is no history of a reaction to the nuts, allergy tests should be interpreted with caution, as children can have a positive allergy test but may tolerate the nut without getting a reaction. Skin prick tests are safe and can be done in a clinic, if antihistamines have not been taken for a few days. Blood tests are not affected by antihistamines. If the diagnosis is uncertain, an oral challenge is sometimes recommended.

- **How can my child avoid tree nuts?**

Cashews, pistachios, almonds, and hazelnuts can be hidden ingredients in food, particularly in Asian, Chinese, and Thai food. Hazelnuts, Brazil nuts, cashews, and almonds can also be found in baked sweets and chocolates.

Unpackaged foods in bakeries and delicatessens sold alongside foods containing nuts may be contaminated with tree nuts and should be avoided. You should read the ingredients list on pre-packaged foods and ask for the chef's reassurance in restaurants. Ringing the food outlet to get information before planning a meal can help avoid any disappointment. Overall, it is often easier to avoid all nuts, than avoid just some nuts.

- **How should you manage a reaction?**

A written management plan given by the specialist will provide all the necessary instructions. Also, allergy medication should be available at all times. If tree nuts are accidentally eaten, get the child to spit it out if possible and give an antihistamine.

Severe reactions include reactions such as difficulty in breathing (wheezing, noisy breathing, and blue colour), swelling in the throat (noisy breathing and drooling), feeling faint or dizzy and looking very pale. In such a scenario, lay the child down with their legs raised and get help straight away and dial 108, stating the cause as anaphylaxis (ana-fil-ak-sis).

***

6. Sesame Allergy

- **What is sesame seed allergy?**

Sesame seed allergy consists of a reaction to sesame protein, after eating the seed. It has become more common over the past ten years and is estimated to affect 1 in 100 people. One in three children with multiple food allergies may have sesame allergies.

- **What are the symptoms of sesame seed allergy?**

Symptoms usually occur straight after eating food containing sesame seeds but can occur up to one hour later. The reaction tends to be mild and may include a rash (hives or 'nettle' rash) or swelling, especially around the face. In some cases, Some children develop an itchy throat, while in some cases, they vomit or have diarrhoea. Severe reactions (anaphylaxis) are less common and include difficulty in breathing (with wheeze or swelling in the throat) and feeling faint or dizzy. People can also develop delayed skin reactions to creams and toiletries containing sesame seed oil.

- **How serious is sesame seed allergy?**

Most people with sesame seed allergy will only have mild reactions. Severe reactions affecting the child's breathing can occur in about 15 per cent of cases, particularly in those with poorly controlled asthma. More severe reactions may also occur if the child has a cold, following intense exercise, at times of stress, or in teenagers after drinking alcohol. Such severe reactions need urgent medical attention.

- **Could a person with a sesame seed allergy also have other food allergies?**

Children with sesame seed allergy may also be allergic to other seeds. They may also be allergic to peanuts and tree nuts. Seek medical advice before excluding any of these foods as it may not be necessary.

- **How do we diagnose sesame seed allergy?**

The diagnosis is based on a history of a typical reaction after contact with products containing sesame. Positive skin prick or blood IgE tests can support the diagnosis, but they should not be used alone, as people can have positive allergy tests but may tolerate the food without getting a reaction.

Skin prick tests are safe and can be done in a clinic, provided that the child has not had any antihistamines for a few days. Blood tests are not affected by antihistamines. If the diagnosis is uncertain, an oral sesame seed challenge is sometimes recommended.

- **How can you avoid sesame seeds?**

Foods containing sesame seeds include tahini, hummus, crackers, breads, bread sticks, burger buns, salads, cereal (health) bars, gomashio, halvah, and falafel. Breads baked in in-store bakeries can also become contaminated with sesame seeds. When eating out, check the ingredients. Middle Eastern, Chinese, Thai, and Japanese foods can all contain sesame seeds. Sesame seeds can also be called juljulan, zelzlane, sumsum, simsim in Arabic, zhī má, hú má in Chinese, goma, shima in Japanese, and til in Hindi, Sanskrit, and Urdu.

- **How should you manage a reaction?**

Children and parents will be given a written management plan in the clinic and prescribed appropriate medication which should be available at all times. If sesame seeds are accidentally eaten, the food should be spat out straight away and an antihistamine should be taken as soon as possible.

- **Who needs to know about this allergy?**

It is important to inform the nursery/school and any after-school clubs. Any other child carers such as grandparents, relatives and school friends' parents will also need to know.

- **Is sesame seed allergy a lifelong condition?**

Most children with sesame seed allergy (over 80 per cent) will not outgrow the problem. If there has been no reaction for a long time and allergy tests to sesame seed come out negative, an oral food challenge can be suggested by your doctor.

- **Is there a cure for sesame seed allergy?**

There is no cure for sesame seed allergy, but research is underway which may lead to the development of new treatments.

***

7. Shellfish Allergy

- **How can my child avoid shellfish?**

Shellfish is easy to avoid. Some foods such as Worcestershire sauce, steak sauce, fried rice, egg rolls, salad dressings, and seafood muffuletta sandwiches can have shellfish as hidden ingredients. Cross-contamination when buying fresh shellfish over the counter in shops and supermarkets can occur. Some dishes like paella, bouillabaisse, gumbo and Frito Misto contain lots of different kinds of fish at once and so, it can be difficult to spot the presence of shellfish. It is useful to avoid such dishes. Some face creams and health supplements can have crushed shellfish.

- **What are the symptoms of fish allergy?**

Symptoms may occur after eating fish, contact with it, or breathing the fish vapour during cooking or at a fish market. Hives or 'nettle' rash or swelling on the face are the most common reactions. Some children have an itchy throat, while in some cases, they vomit or have diarrhoea. Severe reactions are less common but can include difficulty in breathing (wheezing or swelling in the throat) and feeling faint or dizzy. Vapours from the fish may trigger an asthma attack in children who are allergic.

Allergy to fish should not be confused with scombroid poisoning. This is a type of food poisoning that occurs from eating fish that has gone bad. It is more common in warmer countries than in the UK. A chemical (histamine) builds up in the fish as it decomposes, due to which the fish may have a metallic taste and the symptoms are often like those of an allergic reaction.

- **How serious is fish allergy?**

Most people with fish allergy only have mild reactions. Severe reactions affecting the child's breathing can occur, particularly in those with bad asthma and these need urgent medical attention.

- **Could a person with fish allergy also be allergic to other foods?**

People who are fish allergic may be able to eat shellfish. Some people are just allergic to white fish such as cod and haddock but can tolerate salmon and tuna. People allergic to fish need to be aware of the risk of cross-contamination in restaurants, markets, and open fish counters.

- **How to diagnose fish allergy?**

The diagnosis is based on the history of a typical reaction after contact with fish. Positive skin prick or blood IgE tests can support the diagnosis. Skin prick tests are safe and can be done in a clinic, provided that the child has not had any antihistamines for a few days. Blood tests are not affected by antihistamines. If the diagnosis is uncertain, an oral fish challenge is sometimes recommended.

- **Should patients with fish allergy avoid all fish?**

Most patients who are allergic to white fish can eat shellfish. Furthermore, many children who are allergic to white fish such as cod and haddock, can tolerate tuna and sometimes salmon. A possible explanation for this is that different bony fish contain different amounts of the main allergy-causing protein—parvalbumin.

Fish is easy to avoid but watch out for cross-contamination when buying fresh fish in shops and supermarkets. Food fried in oil that has also been used to fry fish will be contaminated. Some foods and dishes like paella, bouillabaisse, gumbo, and Frito misto contain fish and should be avoided, as well as Thai curries with fish sauce and many Japanese fish dishes. Your doctor will advise your child whether they should avoid all fish or just need to avoid white fish and can eat salmon or tuna.

Anisakis is a worm that infects fish in warmer climates (Spain, Italy, Japan, and Korea). It is rare in the UK. If the fish is not properly cooked, it can lead to infection or allergic symptoms in humans. Symptoms include tummy pain, vomiting, and diarrhoea in the case of infection, or allergic reactions (rashes) and even anaphylaxis on repeated exposure. Children allergic to anisakis can eat uninfected fish.

- **How should you manage a reaction?**

After a reaction to fish, your child should be provided with advice about what to do if they have another reaction.

This plan is usually termed as 'allergy management plan'. This plan can be divided into two broad categories:

1. Mild reactions which include hives, swelling, or vomiting, but no breathing problems or faintness. In such a scenario, get the child to spit out the food, if possible. Also, the child should be given an antihistamine.

2. Severe reactions which include difficulty in breathing (wheezing, noisy breathing, blue colour, etc.), swelling in the throat (noisy breathing and drooling), feeling faint or dizzy, and looking very pale. In such a scenario, lay the child down with their legs raised and get help straight away and dial 108, stating the cause as anaphylaxis (ana-fil-ak-sis).

- **Who needs to know about this allergy?**

It is important to inform the nursery/school and any after-school clubs. Any other carers and helpers will also need to know.

- **Is fish allergy a lifelong condition?**

Most children with fish allergy will not outgrow the problem. If there has been no reaction for a long time, an oral challenge may be suggested by the specialist.

2

Cow's Milk Protein Allergy (CMPA)

This chapter deals exclusively with cow's milk allergy since this is the most common allergy in young children. Its presentation, which is difficult to diagnose because of its varied manifestations, has also been explained along with treatment options.

Introduction

Cow's milk protein allergy is one of the most common food allergies encountered in childhood, especially infancy. In positive allergic cases, it becomes quite a challenging task to deal with the nutrition of the child.

Prevalence

CMPA is an allergic condition which is caused by ingestion of cow's milk protein, milk, or other dairy products. There are different protein components in cow's milk, casein, and whey fractions of milk. A child can be sensitised to various proteins singly or in combinations. If it is associated with other food allergies, cow's milk allergy may persist till late adulthood, unlike normal resolution, which happens a lot sooner. Also, a great deal depends on the outcome of the latest test available called component resolved diagnosis.

CMPA occurs in about 5-7 per cent of children who are on formula feeds and this percentage goes down drastically to less than 1 per cent in exclusively breastfed babies. In the latter case, babies tend to have milder reactions and the aspect of being breastfed confers protection against other gastrointestinal disorders as well.

CMPA is more likely to affect children with other atopic or allergic conditions like asthma, allergic rhinitis, and eczema among others as well as children having a history of allergies in their family. Symptoms in CMPA vary and may not strongly present themselves, making the allergy difficult to diagnose.

Diagnosis

Allergic reactions to foods, which fall under adverse food reactions, are usually immune system mediated. Food allergic reactions are an exaggerated immune system response to food protein particles which are usually harmless to the majority of the population. These allergic reactions can be both Immunoglobulin E (IgE) or non-IgE mediated reactions.

IgE Mediated Reactions

Symptoms of IgE mediated reactions occur mostly soon after ingestion of the allergic substance (within minutes to 2 hours). The common symptoms include urticaria and angioedema in skin, vomiting, diarrhoea in gastrointestinal tract, and respiratory symptoms include sneezing, rhinorrhoea, cough, wheezing, and/or chest tightness. Severe allergic reactions, like anaphylaxis, are most likely to occur in children with concomitant poorly controlled asthma.

IgE mediated reactions can be diagnosed with a skin prick test (epicutaneous) or a specific IgE (ImmunoCap). It also helps in prognostication of the outgrowing of food allergies.

Non-IgE Mediated Reactions

As for non-IgE mediated reactions, they generally occur within a few hours to days after consuming milk. Abdominal symptoms are more common which include blood in stools, diarrhoea, and constipation. In infants with persistent colic/gastro-esophageal reflux, CMPA can be considered, if the child is not responding to the standard treatment regimens.

Subtle Reactions

Sometimes the presentation of cows' milk protein allergy may be as subtle as just having anemia along with failure to gain weight without any of the above-mentioned symptoms. It can also present itself with an exacerbation of atopic dermatitis or rarely, just the involvement of the respiratory system with symptoms which may include coughing and wheezing.

In such a scenario, we can establish a causal correlation with cow's milk by excluding it for 2-4 weeks from the baby's diet completely and from the mother's diet, if the baby is on exclusive breastfeeding. If the symptoms get better, then cow's milk can be reintroduced after 4 weeks in the diet again. The cow's milk protein allergy is established if the symptoms recur.

Differential Diagnosis

With an extensive list of symptoms associated with CMPA, the differential diagnosis includes other food allergies, other gastrointestinal disorders, cystic fibrosis, pancreatic insufficiency, and infections. However, the best way to establish if cow's milk is causing these symptoms is to exclude it from the diet. If it's CMPA, there should be an improvement in symptoms within two weeks.

Management through Allergen Avoidance

The yardstick of management of CMPA includes complete avoidance of the allergen. If the CMP is the causative allergen, usually symptoms must resolve within 2 weeks of stopping cow's milk protein.

It is usually recommended to continue breastfeeding during infancy, and if possible, till 2 years of age, to give the child the various benefits of breast milk. In exclusively breastfed babies, the mother is advised to exclude all milk and milk products in her diet and take calcium and vitamin D supplements regularly.

If the child is formula-fed for whatever reasons, extensively hydrolysed milk formulas are advised. They are cow's milk-based but the proteins are broken down to smaller peptides by heat or enzymatic reaction, which are then less likely to elicit an allergic reaction. This may help in balancing growth in children on formula feeds.

If the symptoms persist on hydrolysed formula with a strong clinical diagnosis of CMPA, then a trial of amino acid formula can be given. However, palatability is a limiting factor in many children in this scenario.

Babies who are being weaned and older children with persisting CMPA will need to follow a cow's milk-free diet as above. Parents must be advised about how to check the ingredients of processed foods for milk-derived constituents. Children should be referred to a pediatric dietician for advice about maintaining a balanced diet while excluding allergens.

Oral Food Challenge

The prognosis of CMPA is quite good with a remission rate of approximately 50 per cent at 1 year, about 65 per cent at 2 years, and 80-85 per cent at 3 years. Children may undergo a challenge test every 6-12 months to assess if they will be able to tolerate milk. It may take a few days for the reaction to appear, especially in non-IgE mediated CMPA.

Challenge tests can be done in phases, preferably in a hospital setting, under the supervision of an allergist trained in dealing with possible allergic reactions. Some of the reasons for conducting challenge tests are as follows:

- To assess any allergy to particular foods, if there is ambiguity after a skin prick test or specific IgE.
- To assess tolerance to particular foods.
- In cases where many foods are being avoided in the diet, to guide the parents about reintroducing the foods again in the child's diet.

Usually in CMPA, challenges are done initially with foods containing milk which are least likely to cause reactions and then slowly move towards other foods in order to increase mile tolerance. Baked forms can be tolerated better than uncooked forms. Milk Ladder (mentioned earlier) can be helpful in subsequently doing challenges and reintroducing foods at home after office/ hospital challenges, under the guidance of the treating allergist.

Alternative Milk Sources

Soy formulas have been recommended in the past for the management of children with CMPA. But due to the fact that soy is also a common food allergen, it is not commonly prescribed now. Evidence shows that about 10-20 per cent of children with CMPA have a concomitant allergy to soy as well.

Soy milk also contains oestrogen-like compounds called isoflavones that can adversely affect the immune system. The American Academy of Paediatrics recommends against the use of soy formula for infants because of these isoflavones, even if a child has diarrhoea and CMPA. These isoflavones have a detrimental effect on the growing brain. There is also speculation about the association between soy and the development of ASD/ADHD. Infants and young children who consumed the greatest amount of soy isoflavones had up to a 2.5 times greater chance of developing Kawasaki disease.

Other mammalian milk like buffalo and camel milk is strictly advised to be avoided in children with cow's milk allergy, because of the bio-similarity between cow's milk and other mammalian milk. However, mare's milk is considered the closest to human milk. If it is negative on skin or blood test, it can safely be given after a successful oral challenge test.

Other sources of milk like oats, coconut, or almond may be used after 2 years of age, depending on the child's nutritional status and concomitant allergies. Rice milk is not usually recommended for children under 4.5 years of age. Also, calcium-fortified supplements should be used if possible.

If the symptoms of CMPA tend to persist beyond 4-5 years of age, then patients need to discontinue milk and milk products for a longer period of time, and their nutrition should be addressed under the supervision of a paediatric dietician.

Newer Treatment Modalities

Immunotherapy is a new treatment modality which is being explored in the last few years. Giving increasing doses of milk over a period of time for several months has shown good success rates for children with persisting severe allergies and anaphylaxis.

A Brief Guide for Parents

(As per the recommendations of the NHS England—North West)

- **What Is Cow's Milk Protein Allergy?**

Allergy to Cow's milk protein (CMPA) is one of the leading causes of food allergy in children younger than 3 years. Correct diagnosis helps determine the appropriate diet to be followed, allowing for normal growth and development.

- **What Are Symptoms Related to CMPA?**

The signs of cow's milk protein allergy are varied. It can cause any of the following: difficulty in swallowing, vomiting, food refusal, diarrhoea, rectal bleeding, failure to gain weight, abdomen pain, severe colic, constipation, chronic iron deficiency anaemia, runny nose, wheezing, chronic cough, skin rash, atopic dermatitis, etc. Immediate reactions mainly include vomiting, wheezing, breathing difficulty, urticaria (wheals), swelling of lips/eyelids, severe diarrhoea, leading to collapse, and anaphylaxis (a life-threatening allergic reaction).

- **How Is CMPA Diagnosed and Managed?**

The process of diagnosis includes careful analysis and examination of the patient's clinical history which is followed by skin prick testing (SPT). A blood test for specific IgE and supervised food challenge and elimination are also required in some cases. Children with gastrointestinal manifestations can have negative SPT and IgE, but it does not rule out cow's milk protein allergy.

If CMP allergy is likely, a diagnostic elimination diet for a varying period of time is recommended to look for improvement in symptoms. If there is no improvement in symptoms, CMPA is unlikely.

Some exclusively breastfed infants may develop an allergy to CMP due to protein transfer via breast milk. In such as case, the mother may be asked to go on a strict milk and milk product free diet with calcium supplementation. Non-breastfed babies may have to be started on special milk formulas. Soya protein-based formula may also be recommended after 6 months of age only after soya allergy has been ruled out.

In proven CMP allergy, weaning food should be free of CMP until testing for CMP has been done and a supervised challenge to cow's milk has been performed. If the child does not consume sufficient infant formula, then a calcium supplement will be needed. Cow's milk protein free supplements are generally advised by a registered dietician/doctor. Unnecessary dietary restrictions may result in sub-optimal growth and should be avoided. The input of a trained qualified nutritional expert will be beneficial.

Duration of elimination of cow's milk depends on age, severity of symptoms, and positivity of allergy tests. Retesting and cow's milk challenge should be considered 3 to 12 months after the initial elimination. More than 50 per cent of children are able to tolerate cow's milk by 1 year, 75 per cent by 3 years, and 90 per cent by 6 years of age.

Note: For further information, speak with an allergy specialist, gastroenterologist, and registered dietician.

Case Scenario

Given below is an extract from our publication:

- **Background**

Evidence shows a constant increase in cow's milk allergy in the developing world. In such a case, the alternative sources are either difficult to procure or beyond financial means. Hence, we have looked scientifically at alternate sources available.

In a cross-sectional study, seven children (4 male and 3 female), aged 19 months to 72 months (median age being 40 months) with cow's milk allergy were tested for various milk alternatives. The diagnosis of cow's milk allergy was based on personal history and physical examination and was confirmed by a positive test on component analysis by microtek assay and history. The symptoms reported by the children on ingestion of cow's milk were wheezing (5), atopic dermatitis (4), and urticaria (3).

They were subjected to 300 component analyses using microtek assay and then were challenged with alternative milk options. One child reacted to skin contact also. All were positive for other food allergens and aeroallergens and also had elevated IgE. All seven children were positive for casein components ranging between 0.38 and>50.

The results showed that 6 out of 7 children were negative for mare's milk. 5 out of 7 children were subjected to a direct challenge to mare's milk in an outpatient setting, 1 child was challenged to goat's milk, and 1 child with severe reaction refused all animal milk because they were strict vegans. None of the 5 children reacted adversely to the mare's milk as well as the 1 child challenged with goat's milk. All the 6 children tested successfully for alternate milk were able to continue the alternative milk successfully as on a follow up of one month.

Although the study was small, we could, using microtek assay and with minimal cost and difficulties for the child, diagnose cow's milk allergy components along with the allergy to alternate sources and use this knowledge to conduct a challenge in a proper setting successfully. Mare's milk, if available, can be used as an alternative after a successful challenge (see table on next page).

Salient Points

- It can be tricky to distinguish between the two entities of CMPA and lactose intolerance, but they are actually completely two different conditions.
- A food allergy, such as cow's milk allergy, is an immune reaction to the protein in milk. Lactose intolerance is caused by the inability to break down lactose, which is the sugar in milk.
- It is important to note the presenting complaints and the age of presentation.
- Diagnosis can be done based on the symptoms, either by an SPT or blood tests augmented by an elimination diet and food challenges, if necessary.
- Many children with CMPA tend to outgrow their allergy to milk protein by school going age.

Animal	Component	Case I	Case II	Case III	Case IV	Case V	Case VI	Case VII
		66mo/F	40mo/F	17mo/F	19mo/F	19mo/F	72mo/F	12mo/F
Cow Milk	Bos milk	>50	>50	21	4.1	0.9	Nil	Nil
	Bos d 4 α-Lactalbumin	>50	Nil	Nil	Nil	Nil	Nil	Nil
	Bos d 5 β-Lactoglobulin	>50	1.09	9.6	2.57	1.9	Nil	2.1
	Bos d8 Casein	>50	>50	25	4.0	3.6	0.38	6.0
Camel Milk	Cam d	10.8	8.6	1.1	0.6	0.4	Nil	Nil
Goat Milk	Cap h_milk	33.69	28.92	4.9	0.4	0.3	Nil	0.9
Mare Milk	Equ c_milk	2.17	Nil	1.9	Nil	Nil	Nil	Nil
Sheep Milk	Milk Ovi a_milk	36.23	46.88	8.7	Nil	1.0	0.45	2.0

Case I: Strict vegan who refused animal milk

Case II, III, IV, V, and VII: Participants were challenged successfully with mare's milk in an office setting and were put on mare's milk.

Case VI: The participant was able to tolerate goat's milk.

Alternative Sources for Cow's Milk Protein Allergy M. AHMED1; S. Ahmed1; M. Siddiqi 1 1 Allermy Center For Allergy and Chest Diseases, Hyderabad, India at EAACI, Hamburg 2023.

(The study was awarded the outstanding poster award at the EAACI conference)

3

FOOD ADDITIVES, PRESERVATIVES, AND COLOURANTS

The easy availability of commercial, processed food with additives is the reality of the day, and it definitely has an impact on health, causing many diseases including allergies. It's very difficult to escape it unless one decides to escape to a rural setting. Hence, it is essential that the population should become aware of the content of the food consumed and its probable consequences.

Introduction

It has become a norm to make the food as attractive as possible and to achieve this, colours are added to the food to make it naturally attractive. Also, sometimes food items need to be stored for longer durations and thus, need to have long shelf-life. In such cases, natural preservatives were used in these foods to enable long-term storage. And with the advent of the commercial food industry, preparing food on large scales has become a common practice. This has brought down the cost of foods and resulted in huge profits for the manufacturing units. A traveller who would probably buy freshly made samosas during travel to fill his stomach would now buy a packet of branded potato chips at maybe half the price. Reasons such as doubts about hygiene, content, and quality of ingredients used in locally prepared foods add to the incentive of buying packaged food products. However, packaged food items come laden with preservatives, colouring agents, and additives in order to improve sales and profits. Besides, to make food palatable and desirable, adding high sugar salt and fat becomes a necessity.

Therefore, to have more clarity on the matter, various natural and artificial food substances that are used as additives, preservatives, and colouring agents in foods have been listed below. In addition, the section describes the possible adverse effects that can occur on long-term or excessive use of these substances.

Food Additives

These are substances that are neither normally consumed by itself nor added to food as a typical ingredient. It may or may not have nutritive value and is added intentionally to food to perform a specific technological function.

Direct and Indirect Additives

The functions of direct additives include preserving the food, increasing shelf-life, or inhibiting the growth of pathogens. They are also used to add colour and flavour to improve food palatability, along with texture and appearance. On the other hand, indirect additives are present in food as a result of production, processing, or packing. Also, food fortifiers which are added to food to maintain or improve its nutritive value are not considered as additives.

***

In modern societies, there is a demand for highly palatable and ready-to-serve products. This has resulted in an increase in generalised consumption of industrialised processed foods. And these processed foods always contain additives, preservatives and colouring agents, and artificial flavours apart from fat, salt, and sugars.

In the following sections, we will take a look at the purpose, various types, and harmful effects of additives, and the preventive measures we can take.

Purpose of Additives

Food additives play an important role in ensuring that processed foods remain safe and maintain their quality all through the journey from factories or industrial kitchens to warehouses and shops and finally to consumers. Another important factor is that the food should look attractive and palatable and maintain its nutritive value, and this is also achieved by using additives. They control the acidity and alkalinity of food and thereby regulate the pH value to prevent the growth of bacteria, fungi, or any pathogenic organisms. This, in turn, makes the food cheaper and more convenient to use.

Source

Food additives can be synthetic or be derived from minerals, plants, and animals.

Types of Additives

Natural additives are derived from natural foods such as extracts from beetroot juice, which is used as a colouring agent. The manufactured additives are synthetically produced as a substitute for naturally occurring substances. They are also referred to as artificial additives.

The additives can be further classified as direct and indirect (see above).

Classification of Food Additives

Based on their action, the food additives are categorised as follows:

- Preservatives (E200-299)
- Antioxidants (E300-399)
- Sequestrants (E385 and E386)
- Humectants (E422)
- Bleaching and maturing agents and starch modifiers (E500-599)
- Emulsifiers, stabilisers, gelling agents, and thickeners (E400-499)
- Surface active agents (E400-499)
- Anti-caking and anti-foaming agents (E500-599)
- Colours (E100-199)
- Flavour enhancers (E600-699)
- Acids, bases, and buffers (E300-399)
- Glazing agents (E900-999)
- Artificial sweeteners (E900-999)

Adverse Effects of Food Additives

Some of the immediate effects of food additives include hypersensitive reactions like headache, rashes, hypotension, abdominal pain, vomiting, alteration in behaviour, lack of mental concentration, immunological, and hyperactivity, which is seen more so in children with eczema and asthma.

The long-term effects of food additives include obesity, CVS diseases, type 2 diabetes, degenerative conditions, risk of cancer, endocrine disruption, immune mediated metabolic dysregulation, hyperactivity, exaggeration of ADHD symptoms, not sleeping well, eczema, asthma, dysbiosis, and inflammatory bowel disease.

Why children and adolescents are more susceptible to the adverse effects of food additives?

Some of the reasons why young children are more susceptible to the harmful effects of food additives are as follows:

- They have a higher relative exposure and greater dietary intake compared to adults.
- Their metabolic systems are still developing, and their key organ systems are undergoing substantial changes and maturations due to which they are vulnerable to disruption. Endocrine disrupters are associated with the disruption of the endocrine system in early life, when the developmental programming of organ systems is susceptible to permanent and lifelong disruption.
- Moreover, factors such as advertising, social media trends, and peer pressure have a strong impact during this sensitive period.

Preventive Measures

It would amount to cheating customers if food additives are used to disguise fault-ridden processing and handling techniques. However, sometimes utilisation of additives is unavoidable. Therefore, it becomes important to check food additives for potential harmful effects before usage.

Indian Standards

The Food Safety and Standards Authority of India (FSSAI) is a statutory body established under the Ministry of Health and Family Welfare by the government of India in 2006. It is a statutory body related to food safety and regulation in India. FSSAI is responsible for protecting and promoting public health through the regulation and supervision of food safety. FSSAI decides the quantity of an additive at the lowest level necessary to achieve the intended technical effect.

E-Codes

- E-codes are found on food labels in the European Union.
- An ingredient, which is a food additive, is indicated by E-codes.
- Most countries have their own food labelling laws.

***

1. Direct Food Additives

Preservatives (E200-299)

This category of additives is known as preservatives and they prevent the growth of organisms which could cause food spoilage and lead to food poisoning and sometimes, life-threatening conditions like botulism. They extend the shelf-life of products, so that they can be distributed, sold, and consumed much after their manufacturing date. Many natural preservatives like salt, sugar, vinegar, alcohol, rosemary and oregano extract, diatomaceous earth, castor plant and lemon extracts along with oil and spices are available in India. However, these are not economical and do not extend the shelf-life by a long time.

The chemical preservatives work by adding chemical compounds and through physical methods are dehydration, refrigeration, freeze drying, UV-C radiation, and fermentation. Sorbet/sorbic acid is used as an antimicrobial preservative for the prevention of fungal growth in foods and it can cause urticaria, especially around the mudheap.

Common Chemical Preservatives

Sr	Food	Preservative
1.	Household preservatives	Salt, sugar, vinegar, pepper
2.	Meat, sausages, hotdogs, and smoked fish	Nitrate and nitrites (E251 and E250)
3.	Fruits (inhibit discolouration of cut fruits and serves as anti-browning agent)	Sulphur dioxide and sulphite (E220-228)
4.	Fruit juices, jellies, margarine, carbonated drinks, pickles, and sauces	Benzoic acid and sodium benzoate (E210 and E211)
5.	Provide the acid for flavour improvement in syrups, drinks, and jellies	Citric and tartaric acids (E330 and E334)
6.	Firming agent for pickles and fruit preserves	Alum and soaked lime (HS28333030 and HSN 2522)
7.	Potato chips, breakfast cereals, and canned meats	BHA, BHT (E320, E321), BHA (butylated hydroxy anisole), and BHT (butyrate hydroxyl toluene)

Antioxidants (E300-399)

The oxidation process spoils most food, especially those with a high fat content since fats quickly turn rancid when exposed to oxygen. The antioxidants will prevent or inhibit the oxidation process.

Antioxidants

Sr	Antioxidant	Side Effects	Foods
1.	Ascorbic acid and ascorbate (E 300) Vit C activity	Mostly safe but in some cases, consumption in high quantities may cause renal stones, stomach cramps, headache, and nausea	Citrus fruits, broccoli, and strawberries
2.	Tocopherols (E306, 307, 308, and 309) Vit E activity	Nausea, diarrhoea, stomach cramps, tiredness, and blurred vision	Wheat germ oil, almonds, peanuts, butter, spinach, and sunflower
3.	Gallic acid and sodium gallate (E310) Propyl gallate (phenolic antioxidant)	Skin irritability and allergic reaction	Fruits, nuts, tea, blueberry, grapes, mangoes, and cashew nuts
4.	THBQ (E 319) (tert-butylhydroquinone)	Vision disturbances and liver enlargement neurotoxic	Instant noodles, crackers, doughnuts, popcorn, butter, chicken nuggets, and frozen foods

Preservatives

Sr	Preservative	Side Effects
1.	Sodium benzoate (E211) Carbonated drinks, pickles, and sauces.	Aggravates asthma, allergy, and foetal abnormalities and worsens hyperactivity. It can also act as a neurotoxin and carcinogen.
2.	Sodium nitrite and nitrate (E251) Sausages, hot dogs, smoked fish, and canned meats.	Nitrite is a carcinogen (prostate, breast, stomach, colorectal, neural childhood brain tumours [astroglia]) and can disrupt thyroid functions. Nitrate increases the chances of abortions, foetal deaths, and birth defects. Infants are vulnerable to methemoglobinemia from nitrate and nitrites because of the chemical composition of their gastric tracts.
3.	Benzoic acid (E210) Drinks, low-sugar products, cereals, and meat.	May temporarily inhibit digestive enzyme function and deplete glycine levels. It is better to avoid it in cases of asthma and allergy.
4.	BHA (E320 and 321) and BHT (butylated hydroxy anisole/toluene) Potato chips, vegetable oils, and chewing gum.	These are carcinogenic and toxic to the CNS and liver and can cause behavioural problems and hyperactivity. BHA interacts with nitrites to form chemicals known to cause changes in the DNA of cells and chronic exposure to it can lead reproductive damage.
5.	Sulphur dioxide and sulphites (HSN code 9031, E220-228) Dried fruits and used to prevent brown colouration of cut fruits, breakfast sausages, burger meats, soft drinks, wine, and beer.	Dermatitis, urticaria, hypotension, abdominal pain, aggravated asthma, and diarrhoea.

Colouring Agents (E100-199)

It has become a normal practice to add colour to food and drink. Previously, manufacturers used natural colour compounds of plant and vegetable origin, such as beets (pale red), chlorophyll (green), and extracts of other plants and spices (yellow and orange). Now, the chemical industry has become widespread leading to the inclusion of artificial petroleum-based ingredients for manufacturing artificial food colours. Due to reduced costs and prolonged shelf-life, they are preferred over natural colours.

Colouring agents restore colour lost during the processing or storage stage and thereby, foods, that otherwise would be colourless, are given a colour that makes them more attractive and delectable.

The 6 food colours most closely linked to hyperactivity in children are:

1. E102 (tartrazine)
2. E104 (quinoline yellow)
3. E110 (sunset yellow FCF)
4. E122 (carnosine)
5. E124 (ponceau 4R)
6. E129 (allura red)

Some synthetic colours are made from coal tar or petroleum (the most dangerous additives). These are used to colour beverages, desserts, ice creams, powders, and custards can cause allergies, asthma, hyperactivity, and exacerbation of ADHD.

Flavouring Agents (MSG, BHA, and BHT)

This category of additives comprises natural flavours like spices and their extracts, herbs, roots, essential oils, nuts, and fruit. But a challenge here is that the ingredients from which natural flavours are derived are not available in all the seasons. Due to this reason, natural flavours have now been replaced by synthetic flavour materials like esters, aldehydes, ketones, alcohols, ethers, and smoke flavours of monosodium glutamate. These add flavours to tasteless foods like ice cream jelly and restore the original flavour which may be lost during food processing. For example, monosodium glutamate is added to processed food soups and sauces.

Side Effects of Flavouring Agents

The flavoured foods are hyper-palatable and so we tend to eat more and compromise nutrition. High blood pressure, DNA mutations, obesity, infertility, low testosterone in men, nervous system complications, migraines, allergies, tumours, and accelerated bone loss are some of the side effects associated with flavouring agents.

MSG (Monosodium Glutamate [E621])

The properties of MSG are as follows:

- It is white, odourless, and crystalline powder.
- It is made by fermenting carbohydrate sources like sugar, beet, sugarcane, and molasses.
- It has a specific taste which is known as umami.

The side effects of MSG include obesity, metabolic disorders, brain toxicity, MSC (MSG symptom complex), allergic reactions, and behavioural reactions like headache, weakness, nausea, and altered heart rate. Pregnant women are at increased risk of developing foetus with smaller pituitary, thyroid, and ovary/testes, leading to reproductive dysfunction and stunted growth.

Acids, Bases, and Buffers

They help in altering and controlling the alkalinity or acidity for food safety, taste, and processing and act as a preservative.

E260	Acetic acid	Butter, margarine, fish fingers, and cheese
E297	Numeric acid	Jams, jelly, bread, and fruit drinks
E330	Citric acid	Fruits and vegetables, and soft drinks
E500	Baking soda	Regulates acidity

Glazing Agents (E900-999)

Glazing agents provide a protective coating or a sheen to the surface of foods such as confectionary items, coffee beans, and several fruits including oranges and apples. Some of the commonly used glazing agents are beeswax (E901), camellia wax (E902), and carnauba wax (E903). They may cause allergic reactions and skin irritation.

Artificial Sweeteners (E700-E999)

Artificial sweeteners can be found in frozen desserts, gelatine, desserts, diet soft drinks, yoghurt, and beverages. These substances are carcinogenic, and their side effects include depression, anxiety, seizures, brain tumours, obesity, metabolic disorders like diabetes, CVS diseases, and increasing the release of pro-inflammatory mediators.

Diet Soda/Zero Calorie Version

Diet soda is advertised as a zero-calorie beverage and it is typically sweetened with artificial sweeteners which can cause health problems and contribute to obesity.

***

2. Indirect Food Additives

Insecticides and Pesticides

Insecticides have been associated with ADHD symptoms which are heavily being used on fruits and vegetables. Specifically, researchers found an association between exposure to parathyroid pesticides and ADHD, as well as ADHD symptoms such as hyperactivity and impulsivity. The link between the pesticides and ADHD was stronger in boys than in girls.

Probiotics and Prebiotics

These additives have well-documented benefits for health and well-being. They have a positive effect on the gut microbiota.

Salt (E214-219)

High sodium intake is associated with hypertension, heart disease, and stroke. Industrialised and processed foods' salt content can be as high as up to 500 times more than in a homecooked meal.

Harmful Food Additives

- Sodium nitrite and nitrate
- Aspartame
- Acesulfame
- MSG
- BHA and BHT
- Trans fat
- Colour additives
- Potassium bromates
- Fructose corn syrup (white sugar)
- Olestra
- Propyl gallate
- Sodium chloride

E-Codes to Be Avoided

- E120: Carmine (red colour obtained from the cochlear beetle)
- E129: Allura red (red azo dye)
- E414: Gum Arabic (stabiliser)
- E202: Potassium sorbate (preservative)
- E338: Phosphoric acid (antioxidant sequestrant)
- E621: MSG (flavour enhancer)
- E200: Sorbic acid
- E150: Caramel colour
- E250: Sodium nitrite
- E653: Diasodium ribonucleotide (flavour enhancer)

Difficulties in Monitoring

The number of food additives has mushroomed from about 800 to more than 10,000. And though there are some guidelines specified by authorities, major food conglomerates take advantage of the legal loopholes in food safety laws.

Case Scenario

An 8-year-old child had a past history of wheezing which was resolved by the repeated use of nebulisation. But after a period of three years, the issue presented itself along with repeated rashes on three different episodes when the child had grilled takeaway chicken. During one episode, ER admission was required. However, no adrenaline was needed. Due to these episodes, the parents became concerned about food allergies. The patient tested negative on skin prick and blood tests for chicken and some of the common spices used. The child also never tested positive for home-prepared chicken. Hence, by exclusion, it was confirmed that the cause of the rashes was due to the colourants used in the grilled chicken and the child never got the rashes when eating grilled chicken without colourants. The colourants have now become a common ingredient in foods to make them attractive. The three most widely used dyes are Red 40, Yellow 5, and Yellow 6, and they are known to be carcinogens. Another dye, Red 3, has been acknowledged for years by the Food and Drug Administration to be a carcinogen and yet, it is heavily used in several foods. Research suggests that some children may be susceptible to even tiny amounts of artificial dyes but that a significant number of children were affected by amounts over 35 mg per day. New research has estimated that many children consume over 3-4 times the specified limit of 35mg per day.

Food colourants can sometimes cause allergic reactions and anaphylactic shock. Even natural colouring agents such as annatto, cochineal, and carmine can be potential hazards. An important study, published in the journal The Lancet in 2009, concluded that a variety of common food dyes and preservatives such as sodium benzoate can cause some children to become measurably more hyperactive and distractible. The study also found that the E-numbered food dyes do as much damage to children's brains as lead in gasoline, resulting in a significant reduction in IQ. A yellow colourant (tartrazine), used in soft drinks, energy drinks, cake mixes, salty snacks, cereals, and packaged soups, has been linked to asthma, allergies, and behavioural changes and is banned in some countries. Orange B is banned all over the world but is still used in the US for hotdog and sausage casings. Dyes used in meat, milk, and candies, like Quinoline Yellow, Carmoisine, Ponceau4R, Patent Blue V, and Green S are not allowed in the US and UK.

Salient Points

- Start reading the ingredient labels when grocery shopping.
- Everyone should get habituated to read the FSSAI logo and food labels (FOPL) of packaged foods.
- Try cutting back on processed and packaged foods. Incorporate more fresh ingredients into the diet to minimise intake of food additives.
- Stay away from foods that look unnaturally bright and coloured.
- Fresh homemade food is always preferable.

Section VI
MISCELLANEOUS

1

Food Allergy FAQs

The topic of food allergies tends to raise numerous queries in the mind of an average person. In this chapter, we have tried to cover some general questions pertaining to food allergies. However, some queries may need explanation in a more practical way.

1. **My IgE level is 700 with no allergy issues. What to do?**

   Increased IgE without other symptoms is likely of no clinical significance, although it is surprising that the value is increasing. There was also no mention of eosinophilia. If eosinophilia were present, I would be more concerned about occult parasite diseases such as echinococcal disease or schistosomiasis. In addition, IgE may increase in many non-allergic diseases as well.

2. **My face swells when I eat meat but there are no other symptoms. The allergy test is also negative. What can be the issue?**

   Meat from any kind of mammal—beef, lamb, pork, goat, and even whale and seal—can cause an allergic reaction. While meat allergy is uncommon, there seems to be an increase in the number of cases reported in the past few years and the numbers continue to rise due to increased recognition of the diagnosis.

Another factor to consider is that a lone star tick bite can lead individuals to develop an allergy to red meat, including beef and pork. In such a case, the person needs to be specifically tested for alpha galactose allergy.

3. **After consuming biryani from a restaurant, I experienced a rash, whereas I did not encounter the same reaction with home-cooked food. Is there a specific cause for this?**

   Food allergy to cooked peas—but not raw—has been rarely reported in the literature. In this scenario, the reaction could be due to food additives that may have been used in the outside food.

4. **(i) I ate pomfret in one city but developed a rash in another city. Can this be a food allergy?**

   (ii) I ate fresh fish in Patna from the Ganges but developed a reaction when I ate the same in Goa. Can this be a food allergy?

   ELISA and immunoblotting studies demonstrated that the raw muscle extracts of pomfret, hilsa, bhetki, and mackerel are allergenic but the allergenicity of boiled and fried extracts of pomfret and hilsa was considerably reduced. Reactions can also be elicited due to other factors, such as consuming stale fish.

5. **Can I have an alcohol allergy?**

   Although not a true allergy, in some cases, what seems to be alcohol intolerance might be your reaction to some other ingredient in an alcoholic beverage, such as chemicals, grains, or preservatives. Combining alcohol with certain medications also can cause reactions. In addition, the high histamine content of alcohol can cause rashes.

6. **I experience recurrent cold symptoms that worsen upon consuming citrus fruits and bananas, despite the allergy test yielding negative results. What to do?**

   Bananas are considered a noble food as they fulfil all the energy and vitamin requirements of the body. But since bananas have a mucilaginous texture (sticky and slimy) when mashed, people often associate them as the causative agent in coughs and colds. So, unless a very specific association between eating bananas and the aggravation of cold can be demonstrated, there should be no problem with eating bananas during cough and cold. Also, citrus foods may be traditionally rich in histamine, which may trigger/aggravate the cold and thus, they are labelled as a causative agent for the same.

7. **I develop skin rashes when I take a bath after eating a meal. Additionally, the skin prick tests for the foods I consumed showed negative results.**

   This could be attributed to cholinergic urticaria, a condition in which rashes are induced by a hot shower due to heightened blood circulation in the skin. It also can be a wheat-dependent exercise-induced allergy (WDEIA). See Section II, Chapter 7 for more details.

Salient Points

- As shown from the examples above, all the factors have to be considered when diagnosing food allergies as the reactions/symptoms could arise from a plethora of reasons.
- In case there are additional queries, the reader can forward them to www.allermy.com.

2
The Impact of Food Allergies

Allergy is a chronic condition that significantly impacts the quality of life, both of the patient as well as the family. In this chapter, we detail two case scenarios of food-allergic children, highlighting the impact of the disease. Many parents reading this may correlate it with their own experiences.

Case Scenario 1

Aadya was born in 1999 and delivered by normal vaginal delivery with a birth weight of 2.4 kg. The antenatal and postnatal period was free of any complications. Aadya's parents (both of Indian origin) were non-consanguineous, and she was the eldest child in the family with one younger sister. Her father was a consultant neonatologist in a leading hospital in the UK and the mother was an advocate.

Breastfeeding was initiated immediately after Aadya's birth and she was exclusively breastfed up to four months. The mother was on a normal diet during the breastfeeding phase. Weaning food was introduced just after the fourth month post *annaprashana* (a traditional ceremony). Rice kanji and raagi sari were introduced to Aadya's diet. Later, rice mixed with dal, green grams vegetables, pureed fruits, and white fish to make porridge were also gradually introduced.

In the fifth month, a commercially prepared cereal (Cerelac) was given for the first time with milk solids. She tolerated it well on the first day. However, on the second day, she developed puffiness around the eyes which was noticed immediately after feeding the mixture. Initially, it was attributed to an insect bite or something similar.

The next day, immediately after intake of the cereal, the child developed itchy rashes all around the body along with swollen eyes, lips, and groin. The child was rushed to the hospital and the father being a paediatric trainee, got her treated in the emergency room with intravenous hydrocortisone and chlorpheniramine.

A diagnosis of cow's milk protein allergy was established through clinical assessment, and the family was advised to avoid all milk and milk products, which the parents diligently followed for the next five months, till Aadya was 11 months old.

When Aadya was 11 months old, her dad decided to retest his daughter's allergy. He was trying to give a spoonful of yoghurt but instead, Aadya ended up consuming half of the cup. This caused a massive reaction with body swelling, urticaria, and bronchospasm. She was treated with IV hydrocortisone, IV chlorpheniramine, and nebulisation.

Later, allergen specific IgE antibodies for cow's milk were checked when Aadya was around 5 years of age. The results showed very high readings on many occasions.

The girl had a very good insight about the disease since her childhood, which was helpful for the parents when it came to following a strict trigger avoidance. She wore a tag during her preschool and junior school days which said, 'I am allergic to cow's milk and its products'. She also did not share any food items with her friends.

In 2006, the entire family attended to a conference in Delhi (Aadya was 7 years old at the time) and the hotel staff was informed to prepare a special meal for the child. Later that day, Aadya had paratha and dal curry. Immediately after having the meal, she vomited and this was followed by oedema, urticaria, and bronchospasm. A group of doctors attended the emergency call and there was also an intensivist team on the standby. The family had an emergency medicine bag that contained all the necessary medications and equipment.

A dose of IM adrenaline and nebulisation with salbutamol were given. Aadya showed a quick positive response and did not warrant a hospital admission. She soon recovered fully and enjoyed the rest of her stay with carefully monitored meals.

After this incident, Aadya's parents prepared another bag with all kitchen items to prepare meals inside the hotel and have used it ever since, whenever they go on holidays to both local and overseas destinations.

In 2007, the family shifted to the UK for 2 years for father's postgraduate training. There, Aadya underwent consultation with an allergist who introduced her to an EpiPen. Her teachers were also trained for an emergency but there weren't any frequent reactions during her stay in the UK.

In 2009 (when Aadya was 10 years old), the family shifted to Sri Lanka. During a visit to McDonalds, Aadya had a major reaction after she ate a piece of chicken. EpiPen was used immediately. Since she was negative for other foods that were consumed in the restaurant, this reaction could only be explained the through cross-contamination by the food handlers.

By this time, Aadya's understanding of the disease was much better and she knew that it was a matter of life and death. She understood that maximum avoidance and protection was the only option.

One afternoon, the family was enjoying the afternoon tea and having *aluwa* (a sweet made up of rice flour and treacle) when an incident occurred. As soon as Aadya ate the sweet, she developed swelling, urticaria, and bronchospasm. Her father had to give 2 doses of IM adrenaline and nebulisation at home. But this time, her response was poor, and she collapsed. She was rushed to the main paediatric hospital in Colombo. On admission, she had unrecordable blood pressure, cold peripheries, and was blue with 35 per cent SaO2 in room air. She was admitted to the ICU and required about 12 doses of adrenaline, fluid bolus therapy, and ventilator support for 12 hours. After Aadya made a considerable recovery, she was discharged the next day.

The manner in which the child came into contact with cow's milk remained uncertain. The aluwa consumed was analysed and it came negative for cow's milk. Finally, it was concluded that the piece that the child ate might have been contaminated with a few drops of cow's milk. This showed that the trigger or the severity of the anaphylaxis was not dose dependent.

In another incident, her anaphylaxis was triggered when she shared a soft drink with the same straw. By this time, Aadya was mature enough to recognise her symptoms and use the EpiPen. Later, it was found that a friend in the group who had shared the straw with her had previously consumed ice cream.

Aadya is now 23 years old and has completed her first year of her undergraduate studies in psychology in Sri

Lanka and is now in Canada to complete the degree. And even though she is unable to have chocolates, biscuits, ice cream, yoghurt, cheese, cake, and many other popular food items, and has to carry EpiPen wherever she goes, by and large, she leads a natural and normal life. Some of the significant reasons for her successfully managing her allergy is that she is determined and courageous and has efficiently adjusted her life to face her allergy battle. Also, factors such as her father being a doctor, constant assistance and active guidance from both her parents, belonging to a financially sound family, and having a good insight about the disease have also played a crucial role. Additionally, being in a country like Canada where there is a strict and reliable legal system when it comes to labelling contents of food packs further helps the cause. Currently, Aadya leads a fairly comfortable life in Canada.

***

Case Scenario 2

Sarita married her college friend, Sudhir, who happened to be from her community only. They were also compatible when it came to food habits as both of them were strict vegetarians

A year after marriage, they had a baby girl, Shobha, and the entire family adored her dearly. Shobha was strictly breastfed and when she was 6 months old, the family performed annaprashana, a ceremony wherein relatives gather and the child is given the traditional Telegu food, which is a mixture of rice and dal. The child's grandmother took extra care to prepare the traditional weaning food. This extra care and support from the extended family continued in the future as well.

When Shobha was two years old, the family had to move from Hyderabad to North Carolina in the USA. They didn't have much problem adjusting to the new place because Shobha was now a healthy chubby 2-year-old.

Two years after shifting to the USA, they had their second daughter, Kiran. As before, Sarita breastfed the new baby but due to some feeding issues and lack of domestic help, she transitioned partially to using formula for a month. Kiran didn't take well to the formula feeding and after a month, Sarita started strictly breastfeeding her.

When Kiran turned 6 months old, because of the lack of community support, there was no ceremonial weaning and she was directly started on packaged wheat formula. She did tolerate it well but around 8 months of age, she reacted very badly to her mother's milk. Her reactions included rash, vomiting, and loose motions. Sarita was advised to stop all milk intake while breastfeeding and it did have a positive impact. At the same time, Kiran was developing rashes around her neck, cheeks, and joints.

Sarita wondered why her second daughter had to suffer so much when her elder daughter never had any issues regarding allergies. Though one of the probable contributing factors was that Shobha did get a lot of viral infections that she contracted from her cousins, with whom she had frequent interactions on a regular basis, there was another aspect that differed in the care of the younger one.

During her second pregnancy and nursing period, Sarita was eating a lot of packaged and processed foods because it was easily available and the most cost-effective food around. Also, since she was alone in a foreign country with no help around, it was more convenient for her to wean Kiran on the packaged wheat and rice formula.

As the Kiran rashes continued to worsen, Sarita found herself grappling with numerous challenges. The cost of the moisturiser that had to be used thrice a day, and that too liberally, was eating into the family's already rising expenses. Sudhir too started getting irritated with the whole ordeal. As for Sarita, during the daytime, she had to manage the office stress and at night, she was unable to get proper sleep because of the intense itching. She was prescribed an anti-allergic which didn't help much with the itching but definitely put her to sleep.

After a year of finding no resolution, a consultation was sought with an allergist. This wasn't an easy decision for the family as their routine insurance didn't cover this fee and on top of that, they had to shelve out more money for the tests.

A blood test for food allergies was done and it came positive for multiple foods. The family was strictly vegetarian, and the results further compounded the care in terms of Kiran's diet. Tree nuts such as pistachios, cashew nuts, and walnuts were present at elevated levels, although Kiran was never ever given these foods. The doctor explained to the family that in breastfed babies, the consumption of specific foods can cause such problems. The almond was also highly elevated but since she was consuming almond milk on a regular basis without worsening of symptoms, Kiran was advised to continue. The doctor also advised them to exclude it from Kiran's diet due to positive test results.

The parents continued with their ongoing care for eczema along with restrictions suggested on their diet. They didn't go back to their allergist in the USA since their insurance didn't cover it.

After about two years, they came to India as a part of their annual visit and during this time, they came to me for a consultation. In my examination, I found that the child was having persistent moderate eczema. The prescription was perfect. However, the parents were very concerned about the future. I noticed that the parents were neither counselled in detail about the use of the prescribed drugs nor had any knowledge about how the allergy would progress.

I made them sit down for an hour and explained in detail the intricacies involved in the use of moisturiser and topical steroids. The parent's concern regarding whether the child would develop a fatal reaction like anaphylaxis and whether she would outgrow the disease were also addressed. I informed them about the tests available to confirm the same and shared all the details pertaining to these tests at length. Fortunately, these tests had recently become available, and the parents could get their child tested. Since the child was positive only for the unstable component of peanut and milk, we could confidently convince them to consume peanut and milk in the cooked or boiled form. Unfortunately, this did not hold true for tree nuts since the stable components were positive for tree nuts.

Salient Points

- Food allergies can have a stigma around it and can significantly affect the quality of life of the people who suffer from it as well as their families.
- Food allergy can lead to a lot of unnecessary food restrictions and nutrient deficiencies unless properly guided by an allergist.
- Many cases of food allergies have restricted treatment because of the costs involved.

Appendix I

1

Breastfeeding

Breastfeeding is very important for the prevention of food allergies. In this chapter, we explain its importance and also cover how to initiate and overcome problems related to inadequate milk intake.

Breastfeeding is one of the best gifts that a mother can give to her newborn child. WHO recommends that mothers should exclusively breastfeed infants for the child's first six months to achieve optimal growth, development, and health. Thereafter, they should be given nutritious complementary foods while continuing breastfeeding up to the age of two years or beyond.

There is no doubt that breastfeeding is miles ahead of formula feeding. The formula feed companies encourage bottle feeding if breastfeeding fails. This chapter has been included because all studies have unanimously agreed that exclusive breastfeeding in the first six months substantially decreases the incidence of allergies. Results of this study found a significant inverse association between prolonged breastfeeding (based on the WHO definition) and the prevalence of allergic disease, which suggests a protective effect of breastfeeding from the development of allergy in children living in a poor socio-economic area within a developing country. This protective effect was most pronounced for hay fever, which may be due to the fact that hay fever is an allergic disease that is most strongly associated with atopy.

A striking feature of these results is the observation of an inverse association between breastfeeding duration and the risk of allergic disease in children without an allergic predisposition. A history of allergy in either parent appeared to neutralise the protective effect of prolonged breastfeeding. However, the fact that the inverse association between prolonged breastfeeding and allergic disease was negated by an allergic family history, irrespective of whether it was maternal or paternal, suggests that genetic predisposition is probably the overriding factor.

The mechanisms responsible for the protective effect of breastfeeding against allergic disease are not well understood, but several factors may contribute to this phenomenon including the hygiene hypothesis.

In spite of adequate evidence highlighting the benefits of breastfeeding, there are many reasons due to which a mother might not be able to breastfeed. Hence, their doctors have to work out a suitable solution depending on the problem.

Important Facts About Breastfeeding

The initial milk secreted during breastfeeding is called colostrum, and it is present in a very small quantity and thus might give a perception of inadequate milk. Colostrum is full of antibodies and has enough calories for the baby. If prelacteal feeds are given, then the baby will have less interest in breastfeeding since the hunger has been overcome. Also, the sucking of the nipple with consequent nerve stimulation causes the oxytocin reflex to produce more milk. Thus, breastfeeding should be started at the earliest. In a caesarean section baby, the feeding can be started as soon as the mother is off anaesthesia. In this case, the mother can breastfeed while lying on her back and in side position when possible. This, however, will need more assistance from the caregivers.

The most common problem mothers express when it comes to breastfeeding is that they aren't getting enough milk. More often, this is generally a misconception. Nonetheless, they need to be referred to a nursing consultant to check for proper and adequate latching.

While feeding, the baby should be fed on one breast only to make certain that the baby gets the foremilk which is adequate in water and the hindmilk which is rich in fats. The size of the breast has no relation to the amount of milk secreted. Also, if there is any breast pain during feeding, then this is not related to the process of breastfeeding and has more to do with poor latching.

Also, excessive crying of the child is not always due to hunger or inadequate milk. There are many other physiological reasons which need to be attended to by the physician in such a case. An interesting point is that formula-fed babies sleep longer because formula feed takes longer time to digest while breastfed milk is digested faster, necessitating the need for frequent feeding.

When it comes to diet, breastfeeding mothers can have all kinds of food including dairy products, unless the baby has a particular allergy, especially milk related. One important thing is that breastfeeding mothers should set a limit on the consumption of tea, coffee, and alcohol.

I will conclude this chapter with the biggest myth concerning breastfeeding and it is that a working mother cannot breastfeed. The truth is that working mothers can continue breastfeeding. She can breastfeed before going to work and after coming back from work. She can also express her milk for occasions when she cannot breastfeed. Expressed milk can remain at room temperature for 4 to 6 hours and at 4 degrees Celsius in the refrigerator for 24 hours.

Salient Points

- Breastfeeding is the best option for a newborn and there are no alternatives that are as nutritional and healthy.
- When it comes to breastfeeding, keep trying till you succeed.

2

Traditional Indian Weaning Diets

The Indian subcontinent is an agglomeration of different caste religions tribes and societies in existence. Over the years, with observations and experiences, they have developed many practices, some with religious and some without religious connotations. Some of these practices have also been scientifically validated. In this chapter, we cover some of these practices and explain their importance.

Introduction

In India, there are we have sixteen *sanskars*. The prefix 'san' translates to Good and 'kar' has been derived from the word *karya*, which means work. Thus, the word sanskar translates to 'good work'.

Annaprashana

Annaprashana is one of the sixteen sanskars, and it is done when the baby turns 6 months old as a celebration of the first half-yearly birthday. Also, as covered in the previous chapter, mother's milk should be fed to the child at least up to the age of 6 months as it provides the necessary nutrients for the all-round development of the baby. After that, to keep pace with the rapid growth, additional semi-solid or solid food is required.

From time immemorial, it has been accepted that rice is the best choice of food for the baby to start with as it is a good source of carbohydrates, can easily be simplified, and supplies instant energy to the body. In Sanskrit, boiled rice is called 'anna' and hence, the word 'annaprashan' which means the 'first rice intake'.

The reason this period is significant is because at the age of 6 months, the baby's body gets ready to digest solid foods, their first tooth appears, and the enzyme secretion also begins. They slowly gain the ability of sustenance with staple food. Therefore, the ceremony of annaprasan holds a special significance both for the baby and the family. It marks the transition of the child's food from liquid to semi-solid or solid, from exclusively feeding breast milk to staple food.

This celebration differs from place to place, person to person, and family to family. Some observe it with much pomp and show, some more intimately, and some with much devotion. A pooja is conducted and kheeri is prepared, which is first offered to God after which, and then it is given to the baby.

Some important pointers to be kept in mind are as follows:

- Kheeri must be prepared with only rice and milk along with a little jaggery and pure ghee.
- It must be properly boiled and prepared hygienically. The feeding bowl and the spoon must be properly sterilised. Usually, new spoons and bowels are used for the purpose.
- The person feeding the baby must wear clean clothes and wash their hands thoroughly.
- Over-feeding must be avoided.
- Over-crowding can be detrimental and must be avoided as far as practicable.

- The ceremony must be observed when the baby is 6 to 8 months old.
- After the first feeding, the quantity of the solid food must be increased gradually, but breastfeeding should not be stopped.

For many decades, Western society had been promoting formula feeding and late weaning. Whether it had any true scientific basis or was industry driven by the baby food industry is a matter of conjecture. However, now the Western medical recommendations have returned to the unquestionable value of breastfeeding, especially breastfeeding exclusively for the first six months. As far as weaning is concerned, there is the LEAP (learning early about peanut allergy) study from Germany (see illustration on next page), which suggests the early introduction of peanuts in infants who have a family history of peanut allergy in order to prevent the development of peanut allergy. This is exactly what Indians have been doing traditionally.

There have been numerous studies in the West regarding weaning foods and the timing of weaning. The Western medical model was earlier advocating the late introduction of high protein-containing foods. There is not only a difference in the time of weaning and the type of food but even reputable organisations such as AAP (American Academy of Paediatrics) policy recommendations of each decade have shown vacillations in contrast to a steadfast commitment to breastfeeding in the Indian traditions.

In many ancient scriptures as well, it has been advocated to breastfeed for the first two years of a child's life. If the mother cannot breastfeed for some reason, then a wet nurse can be advocated. It is akin to today's milk bank. However, at no stage, supplemental feeds is advocated in the first six months.

LEAP Study Results

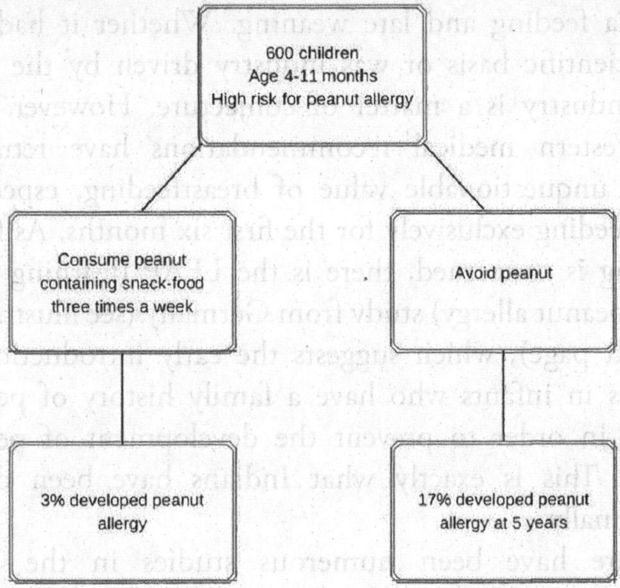

Note: Based on the hypothesis that regular eating of peanuts, when started during infancy, will elicit a protective immune response instead of an allergic immune reaction.

Salient Points

- It is always best to go back to basics.
- Traditional methods should be adhered to, if they have stood the test of time.

3

Master Chef Recipes

In the contemporary world, many mothers, especially those who are working, are not well aware of what all can be given to babies as complementary feeds. Many resort to packaged stuff from supermarket stores as they are advertised on electronic media. This chapter provides some simple, easy-to-cook, and healthy recipes for mothers.

Savoury Recipes

1. Oats Pancake

Oats pancake is savoury food full of nutrients and easy to digest. Oats contain a very high amount of iron, magnesium, fibre, and zinc which helps in digestion and prevent constipation. It can be introduced as a solid food for 6-months-old babies.

Ingredients

- Oats powder: 1 cup
- Curd: ½ cup
- Grated carrots: 1 tbsp
- Grated tomatoes: 1 tbsp

- Grated panner: 1 tbsp
- Vegetables are optional and can be used as per choice.
- Carom seeds (ajwain) for digestion: ¼ tsp
- Himalaya pink salt or sendha namak to taste
- A pinch of turmeric
- Ghee for cooking

Health Properties

- Turmeric is anti-allergic and improves immunity.
- Ghee helps in the development of bone, skin, and metabolism and also improves the taste of food.
- Sendha namak is the healthiest salt as per Ayurveda. It contains minerals and is free of all chemical processing.

Method

- Mix all ingredients together and adjust consistency with water, if required.
- Heat the tawa and grease with ghee.
- Spread a spoonful of batter on hot tawa.
- Flip the pancake once it becomes golden brown.
- Serve with curd or any homemade mild chutney.

***

2. Green Sprout Chilli/Dosa

Green sprouts are full of nutrients. It is high in protein, carbohydrates, fibre, and omega-3 fatty acids. It helps in building muscle and bone and promotes body growth.

Ingredients

- Moong sprout: 1 cup
- Gram flour (besan): 1 tbsp
- Cumin seeds: 1 tsp
- Chopped onion, tomatoes, and coriander leaf: 1 tbsp (for filling)
- Paneer: 1 tbsp (for filling)
- Himalaya pink salt or sendha namak to taste
- Ghee: 1 tsp

Health Properties

- For filling: Mix grated paneer, grated carrot, finely chopped coriander, and salt to taste in a bowl and keep aside.

Method

1. Finely grind the sprout and in this mixture, add gram flour, cumin seeds, and salt to taste.
2. Mix it well with all the ingredients mentioned above.
3. On the hot tawa, grease some ghee and spread the batter like a dosa or chilla. Cover it with a lid and cook on both sides.
4. Now spread paneer filling on top of it and roll the dosa.
5. When serving, cut the roll into pieces and serve with any homemade chutney or curd.

***

3. Chickpea Cutlet (Protein Cutlet)

Chickpea is one of the superfoods. It's a rich source of vitamins, minerals, fibre, and protein.

Ingredients

- Boiled chickpeas: 1 cup
- Boiled potato: 1
- Blanched vegetables (carrots, beans, cauliflower, or any other vegetable of choice)
- Ghee: 1 tbsp
- Himalaya pink salt or sendha namak to taste
- A pinch of turmeric
- Sesame seeds for upper coating of cutlets

Health Properties

- Sesame seeds are a good source of iron, calcium, and zinc and also full of protein and fibre. These ingredients are often low in toddlers' and infant's diets.

Method

1. Mash all the ingredients together (boiled chickpeas, potatoes, and vegetables).
2. Add salt and turmeric and form a dough.
3. Form any shape with the help of palms and coat it with the sesame seeds.
4. Heat the ghee on the pan or tawa and cook both sides, till it becomes golden and crispy.
5. Serve with homemade curd or any chutney.

***

4. Quinoa

Quinoa is a pseudo-grain that is very good for toddlers or babies and can be introduced at the age of six months. It is very rich in antioxidants and is also a great source of protein, iron, and omega-3 and 6 fatty acids.

Ingredients

- Quinoa: ½ cup
- Curd: ¼ cup
- A pinch of Himalaya pink salt or sendha namak

Method

This recipe can made in multiple ways with different ingredients.

1. Take ½ cup of boiled quinoa. Add ¼ cup of fresh homemade curd and a pinch of sendha namak or Himalaya pink salt and mix it well. The consistency can be adjusted by adding water.
2. Take ½ cup of boiled quinoa. Add ¼ cup of cooked daal instead of curd and mix it well. The consistency can be adjusted by adding more daal.

***

Sweet Based recipes

1. Homemade Cerelac

Nowadays, readymade and packed foods are a very convenient option for all mothers. But the issue is that these packed foods are full of preservatives and artificial sugar, which can be very harmful in the long run.

Here is the recipe for homemade porridge that can prepared easily and quickly. It can be stored in a container and is also travel friendly.

Ingredients

- Roasted rice: 1 cup
- Roasted channa daal: 1 cup
- Roasted fox nuts or lotus seeds (makhana): 1 cup
- Roasted poha: 1 cup
- Roasted cashew nuts: ¼ cup
- Roasted almond: ¼ cup
- Elachi powder: 4-5 pods
- Jaggery powder or dates powder for sweetening

Health Properties

- Fox nuts or lotus seeds contain high fibre and help prevent constipation in toddlers and babies. They are also a good source of calcium which helps in strengthening the teeth and bones.
- Dry dates powder is an excellent source of natural laxative that helps in preventing constipation and also a good source of vitamin A, calcium, and magnesium which, in turn, boosts immunity.

Method

1. Dry roast all the grains and nuts separately.
2. Cool them completely and grind them into powder.
3. Mix all the powder and keep in an airtight container.

Preparation

Take 2 tablespoons of the powder (mentioned above) in a pan and add 1 cup of water or milk. Remove all the lumps and mix them well. Cook on medium flame by continuously stirring for 5 minutes or till it gets a porridge consistency. Add jaggery powder or dated powder for sweetening. It can be fed to 6 to 12 months old babies as a staple food.

***

2. Sweet Oats Pancake

Ingredients

- Oats: 1 cup
- Semolina: 1 tbsp
- Nuts powder: 1 tbsp
- Jaggery powder or dry dates powder: 1tsp
- Ghee: 1 tbsp
- Honey
- Fruits (optional)

Health Properties

- Honey gives energy and also helps with coughs.
- Ghee helps in the development of bone, skin, and metabolism and also improves the taste of food.

- Fruits help boost the immune system and prevent infections. They also contain a good amount of potassium, minerals, vitamin C, vitamin A, and fibre.

Method

1. Dry roast oats in a pan and grind them into powder.
2. In a bowl, take 1 cup of powdered oats and add 1 tablespoon of semolina.
3. Now add nuts powder, jaggery powder, and milk to make a paste with thick consistency.
4. Heat the tawa and grease with the ghee.
5. Put 1 tablespoon paste on it but do not spread much.
6. Based on the desired softness and fluffiness of the pancake, put some ghee on it and flip both sides till it gets cooked.
7. Serve it with honey or maple syrup. Some cut seasonal fruits or grated fruits can also be included.

***

3. Apple Porridge or Halwa

Ingredients

- Apple: 1
- Ghee: 1 tsp
- A pinch of cardamom (elaichi powder)
- Nuts powder: 1 tbsp
- Soaked chia seeds: 1 tbsp

Health Properties

Chia seeds provide multiple benefits. They contain omega-3 fatty acids which help in the growth and development of muscles. They also contain fibre, which improves the functioning of the digestive system, as well as calcium, zinc, and manganese help in the proper maintenance of tissues and strengthening of bones and the immune system.

Method

1. Grate an apple.
2. Take a pan with 1 teaspoon ghee, add grated apple, and sauté for 2 to 3 minutes.
3. For nutrition, add 1 tablespoon of mixed powdered nuts and a pinch of cardamom powder for flavouring.
4. This recipe doesn't need any extra sweetener as cooking the apple increases its sweetness.
5. For serving, take a bowl, add apple halwa, and top it with 1 tablespoon of soaked chia seeds to add extra nutrition.

***

4. Raagi Porridge/Raagi Malt

Raagi is a superfood for babies and toddlers. It's very good for their appetite and digestion as its gluten free. It also helps in strengthening bones as it contains a high amount of calcium which no other cereal can provide.

Ingredients

- Raggi: 2 tbsp
- Ghee: 1 tsp

- Milk or water: 1 cup
- Jaggery powder or dry dates powder: 1 tsp

Method

1. Take a pan and dry roast raagi.
2. Add water or milk gradually.
3. Stir continuously to make sure no lump forms.
4. Add ghee and jaggery and the dish is ready.

Salient Points

- Try to use as much as much natural foods and ingredients as possible.
- Avoid salt and sugar as much as possible.
- Millet should be incorporated into the diet due to their multiple health benefits.

Appendix II

1
JUNCS Food

The world has witnessed significant advance in all sectors which has completely revolutionised the way we live our life. The development of food industries has also brought about an immense change in our eating habits. This, in conjunction with the modern lifestyle, has led to a long chain of health disorders, termed lifestyle diseases. Allergy, especially food allergy, is an offshoot of this deviation in food habits.

Introduction

In the last two decades, there has been an exponential rise in the consumption of fast foods and sweetened beverages in Indian children. In the modernised world, easy availability, convenience of eating, high palatability, attractive presentation of the product with catchy advertisements, lower cost, and extensive marketing along with working parents are some of the major factors for the high consumption of these products.

The major adverse effects pertaining to the intake of fruit juices and fast foods are obesity and associated complications, allergies, microorganism contamination leading to infection, and risk of cancer due to carcinogenic and allergenic properties of some food additives. In the following sections, we will discuss the various kinds of JUNC foods, their harmful effects, and some guidelines that should be followed in such an ecosystem.

Definition and Identification of Undesirable Food and Drink Items

1. **Fast Food**
   This category includes foods designed for ready availability, use, or consumption with little consideration given to quality or significance. Salads and cut fruits are included in this category and therefore, all fast foods need not be unhealthy. Also, certain foods such as oats and cornflakes, which are marketed as healthy foods may actually be unhealthy as they may have a lot of colours and additives. Similarly, pickles which generally are not considered unhealthy, may be made with a lot of oil or dalda. Hence, it is important to be mindful of what we are feeding our bodies.

2. **Junk Food**
   These are foods (packed or non-packed, processed or not processed) which contain no or little essential healthy ingredients such as proteins, vitamins, phytochemicals, minerals, and dietary fibre, and instead, have high amounts of fat (saturated fatty acids), salt, sugar, and calories. These foods can have a negative impact on health if consumed regularly or in high amounts. Some of the commonly used products in Indian homes belonging to this category are maida, sugar, oils, besan or gram flour, dalda, vanaspathi oil, and khova.

3. HFSS Foods

These foods are also high in fats, salt, or sugar content but they lack popularity among the lay public.

4. Ultra-Processed Foods

This category, by definition, does not include homemade or freshly prepared food and uses ingredients that are mainly used for industrial processing. These substances are generally broken-down using chemicals and have added colourants and flavours and by the end, there are undesirable nutrients and/or toxins. This makes foods in this category more hyperpalatable and thus, more obesogenic.

Barley malt	Coconut sugar	Golden sugar	Maltose	Raw sugar
Beet sugar	Corn syrup	Golden syrup	Mannose	Rice syrup
Brown sugar	Date sugar	Grape sugar	Maple syrup	Sorghum syrup
Buttered syrup	Dextrin I	Cine sugar	Molasses	Syrup
Cane juice	Dextrose	Invert sugar	Muscovado	Saccharose
Cane sugar	Fructose	Malt syrup	Palm sugar	Sucrose
Caramel	Fruit juice	Malt dextrin	Panocha	Treacle
Carob syrup sugar	Glucose	Maltol	Refiner sugar	Yellow sugar

5. JUNCS

This category consists of junk foods, ultra-processed foods, nutritionally inappropriate foods, caffeinated/

coloured/carbonated foods and beverages, and sugar-sweetened beverages. It is a terminology coined by the working group of the Indian Academy of Paediatrics to deal with unhealthy foods.

A Rising Issue

Data from all developed countries shows an increase in the consumption of fast foods and the countries leading this list are the UK and USA. A pan-India survey revealed that almost every child consumed packaged sugar-sweetened beverages, salted packaged foods, and sweet packaged food. This tendency is secular and spread across all socioeconomic groups. The most common junk food items consumed are samosa, manchurian, burgers, patties, noodles, pizza, chips, chocolate, bakery products, soft drinks, sugar-sweetened beverages, and caffeinated drinks.

Factors for Increased Consumption of Junk Foods in India

1. Favourable Demographics

India has a high percentage of young population and the largest working-age population (15-54 years) which is further predicted to rise by 135 million by 2022.

2. Increasing Urbanisation

In 2015, India became the second-largest urban community in the world after China.

3. Growth of Women Workforce

Due to significant growth in the numbers of working women, there has been a decline in homecooked meals and a rise of 'out of home' food trends.

4. Growing Middle Class

There has also been a growth of the middle-class segment, leading to more spending capacity on outside food.

5. Nuclear Family

As per the 2011 census, there has been an increase in urban households having less than five members. A fall in the average household size, coupled with rising disposable income, will lead to greater discretionary spending, including eating out of home.

6. Online Delivery/Digitalisation

Growth in the popularity of online platforms where people can easily order food from any restaurant and instantly get it delivered.

7. Changing Consumer Preferences

More and more people are preferring to eat out and indulge in the vast choices available in the market. Also, the growth of food retail chains in all locations and extensive marketing strategies are other factors leading to the growth of the fast-food industry in India.

Harmful Effects

1. Nutritional Imbalance

The studies have shown that nearly half of the daily average dietary energy in children comes from ultra-processed food. As the contribution of ultra-processed foods to total energy increases, the dietary contents of carbohydrates, free sugars, total and saturated fats, and sodium also increase. This has an inverse relation with the dietary content of protein, fibre, potassium, minerals, and vitamins.

2. Overweight/Obesity

Processed and packaged food is a well-known culprit for the majority of overweight and obesity cases. This issue is further compounded by sweetened and carbonated beverages.

3. Cardiometabolic Risk

Studies have shown a positive association between ultra-processed diet and cardiometabolic alterations in children and adolescents such as an increase in total and LDL cholesterol concentrations and an increase in insulin resistance.

4. High Blood Pressure

Studies show inconsistent results regarding the association between fast food consumption and hypertension in children and adolescents.

5. Behavioural Symptoms

It is hypothesised that unhealthy diets affect mental state and brain function through oxidative stress processes, inflammation, and stress response systems, while vitamins, antioxidants, beta-carotene, and minerals in fruits and vegetables are associated with lower levels of inflammation and oxidative stress.

Existing Recommendations, Guidelines, and Policies

Fast Food

The dietary guidelines on permissible amounts of fats, carbohydrates, protein, free sugar, salt, and micronutrients are available in more than 60 countries. World Health Organization and Dietary Guidelines for Americans (2015-2020) limit intake of free sugars to less than 10 per cent of total energy intake. The Science Advisory Committee for Nutrition (SACN) from the UK (2015) and the ESPGHAN Committee on Nutrition (2017) recommended free sugar intake of 5 per cent or less of the total dietary intake for adults and children aged over two years. WHO and US dietary guidelines recommend that total fat should not exceed 30 per cent of total energy intake, saturated fatty acid intake should be <10 per cent of total energy intake, and trans fatty acids to be <1 per cent. Further, salt intake should be less than 5 g/d (2 g/d sodium).

Advertisement and Marketing

The United Kingdom in 2006 banned advertisements of foods high in fat, sugar, and salt (HFSS) in television programs made for children aged 4-15 years. The same measure has been taken by many other developed as well as developing countries. Some countries like Denmark, Hungary, and France have introduced economic policies as recommended by the WHO in 2008. The United States in 2014 mandated that schools will no longer be allowed to sell unhealthy junk food and SSBs in their cafeterias, vending machines, or student stores. In 2015, the Delhi High Court set a ban on the sale of HFSS food including sugar, sweetened, carbonated, and non-carbonated beverages within the school or within 50 meters of its premises.

Fruit Juices

American Academy of Paediatrics (AAP) has recommended no fruit juices for children below 12 months of age. Fruit drinks are thought to be a good source of minerals and hence inappropriately used in diarrhoea cases, but the fact is that they are not balanced fluids for this condition and can rather aggravate diarrhoea. They may even cause diarrhoea in toddlers by increasing osmolarity.

Fruit drinks are a common cause of tooth decay and promote picky feeding. Unpasteurised juices can be a source of serious bacterial infections. Changes in bowel habits, i.e., abdominal distension, flatulence, and diarrhoea are frequently observed with fruit drinks. This is because of carbohydrate malabsorption as these juices have a high quantity of sorbitol which is nonabsorbable and has high fructose-glucose ratios. Therefore, whole fruits are recommended instead as they supply fibres and phytochemicals to the diet. They also promote extra skills in children like peeling, chewing, and differentiating between colours, textures, and shapes.

Food Labelling

USFDA has directed that any juice reconstituted from pulp must be mentioned on the label and must list the percentage of all the other ingredients. In the UK, fruit juices must not be labelled with 'no added sugar' claim and sugar must not be added to fruit juice. Also, the words 'containing naturally occurring sugars' must also appear.

Energy Drinks

American Academy of Paediatrics and the American College of Sports Medicine (ACSM) have stated that energy drinks are not intended for children and adolescents and are also not recommended before and after strenuous activity. They also advise against mixing energy drinks with alcohol. Water is advocated as the main source of hydration, even during exercise. European Food Safety Authority (EFSA) has concluded that a maximum caffeine intake of 3 mg/kg/d (maximum 200 mg/d) can be considered safe for children and adolescents.

Labelling

All energy drinks should have the advisory statement stating 'not recommended for children or pregnant or breastfeeding women' or similar. Further, the European Union Soft Drinks Association (UNESDA) has asked that the statement must be placed in the same field of vision as the name of the beverage, followed by a reference to the caffeine content expressed in mg per 100 ml.

American Beverage Association (ABA) recommends that the marketing of energy drinks should not be permitted to children younger than 12 years of age. Any image of children on the company website and advertisement in media where the target audience is children is also prohibited. No commercial promotion is permitted in primary and secondary schools and within 100 meters. European Union also does not permit marketing or sampling in audiences where more than 35 per cent are children less than 16 years of age. In India, FSSAI has recommended that non-alcoholic beverages with caffeine content more than 145 mg/L of caffeine will be labelled as 'caffeinated beverage' and caffeine content in these beverages should not cross 300 mg/L, irrespective of the source of the caffeine.

Guidelines and Recommendations of the Indian Academy of Paediatrics

I. Guidelines for Children and Families

- Consumption of JUNCS foods and beverages should be avoided by all children and adolescents, as far as possible.
- Alternatively, limit consumption of JUNCS foods at home/outside. It is also suggested to have no more than one serving per week and the serving should not exceed 50 per cent of the total daily energy intake for that age.
- Do not consume food while watching television/screen.
- Eliminate trans fats and reduce free sugars to <5 per cent of total energy intake.
- Freshly cooked home foods with minimal addition of sugar and no trans fats should be preferred over restaurant/packaged foods.
- Traditional and acceptable homemade snacks with long shelf life can be offered to children as alternatives to JUNCS foods.
- Lunch boxes packed only with healthy food should be carried to school if the school does not have the provision for providing healthy mid-day meals.

The JUNCS food should not be offered as a reward/gift to any child as this gives undue promotion to unhealthy foods.

II. Fruit Juices

- Encourage intake of regional and seasonal whole fruits over fruit juices in children and adolescents.
- Fruit juices/fruit drinks/SSBs should not be offered to infants and young children aged below 2 years.
- For children and adolescents between 2-18 years of age, fruit juices, fruit drinks, and SSBs should be avoided as far as possible. Water should be encouraged as the best drink and should be promoted over fruit juices/drinks at home and school.
- Fruit juices/drinks, if given, should be limited to 125 ml per day for children aged between 2-5 years, and 250 ml per day for age >5 years, and these should preferably be given as fresh juices.

III. Caffeinated drinks

- Caffeinated energy drinks should not be consumed by children and adolescents. Intake of carbonated drinks, tea, and coffee is to be completely avoided by children <5 years.
- In school-going children and adolescents, tea/ coffee intake should be limited to a maximum of half a cup/day (100 ml) in 5-9 years, and one cup/day (200 ml) in adolescents (10-18 years) provided that no other caffeinated products (cola, chocolates, etc.) are being consumed.

Labelling, Advertising, and Marketing

I. Guidelines for Schools

- IAP supports the Ministry of Women and Child Development recommendations to ban the sale of HFSS foods in school canteens and in the near vicinity of 200 meters radius (LOE 5).
- Efforts to regulate availability of the JUNCS foods in schools must be coupled with ensuring the availability and affordability of a variety of healthy snacks and foods in mid-day meals or school canteens (LOE 1b).
- School authorities should ensure the availability of safe and potable drinking water in schools to reduce the consumption of SSBs (LOE 2a).
- Ensuring ongoing support, provision of resources, monitoring, feedback, and recognition will help to increase the compliance of schools to provide healthy food to children (LOE 1b).

II. Guidelines for Labelling

- Supports and advocates traffic light coding of all packaged food as suggested by FSSAI. Labelling of the nutritional content of packaged foods should be further strengthened.

III. Guidelines for Advertisements

- Advertisement of the JUNCS foods may lead to unhealthy food choices (LOE 1a) and is likely to be associated with increasing obesity (LOE 2a).

- Recommends legal ban of screen/print/digital advertisements of all JUNCS foods for channels/magazines/websites/social media catering to children and adolescents through legislative measures.
- Recommends ban of branding and use of licensed characters for promoting fast foods/SSBs.
- Advertisements ridiculing healthy foods need to be legally banned.
- Recommends screen/print/digital advertisements promoting healthy foods for channels catering to children and adolescents and use of licensed characters for branding and promoting healthy foods.

Salient Points

- Eat natural foods as much as possible.
- Avoid junk and coloured foods.
- Juices are to be avoided in the first two years.
- Caffeinated drinks in children are a strict no.
- Don't get carried away by health drink advertisements even if it is endorsed by your favourite star/celebrity.
- The government cannot keep banning various food items but provides advisories which need to be taken seriously.

Appendix III

1

Nutrition Guidelines by the National Institute of Nutrition

The internet is full of ideas and suggestions about what to eat and not eat. To overcome this dilemma, we present the NIN guidelines which is a premier institute of nutrition in India.

Introduction

The Indian subcontinent is home to 1.8 billion people and the population itself is very diverse. The middle-class population in India is the same as the population of the USA, amounting to 350 million and is growing. At the same time, especially in rural areas and in urban slums, there are vast swathes of population who are denied clean drinking water and suffer from malnutrition. In such a diverse and varied country, the same guidelines applicable to the developed world cannot be applied.

Hence, the National Institute of Nutrition has come up with a set of 15 guidelines and points to keep in mind in our day-to-day lives. There may be some differences in certain aspects of nutrition, however, readers need to understand that these guidelines have been formed by experts who have been working at the field level and have thoroughly taken into consideration the pros and cons of each guideline.

Guideline 1: Eat a variety of foods to ensure a balanced diet.

Rationale

A nutritionally adequate diet should be consumed through a variety of foods.

- Nutrition is a basic prerequisite to sustain a healthy life.
- Variety in food is not only the spice of life but also the essence of nutrition and health.
- A diet consisting of foods from several food groups provides all the required nutrients in proper amounts.
- Cereals, millet, and pulses are major sources of most nutrients.
- Milk, which provides good-quality proteins and calcium, must be an essential item of the diet, particularly for infants, children, and women.
- Oils and nuts are calorie-rich foods and are useful for increasing the energy density and quality of food.
- The inclusion of eggs, flesh foods, and fish enhances the quality of the diet. However, vegetarians can derive almost all the nutrients from diets consisting of cereals, pulses, vegetables, fruits and milk-based diets.
- Vegetables and fruits provide protective substances such as vitamins, minerals, and phytonutrients.
- Diversified diets with a judicious choice from a variety of food groups provide the necessary nutrients.

Points to Keep in Mind

- Choose a variety of foods in amounts appropriate for age, gender, physiological status, and physical activity.
- Use a combination of whole grains, grams, and greens. Include jaggery or sugar and cooking oils to bridge the calorie or energy gap.
- Prefer fresh, locally available vegetables and fruits.
- Include in the diet foods of animal origin such as milk, eggs, and meat, particularly for pregnant and lactating women and children.
- Adults should choose low-fat, protein-rich foods such as lean meat, fish, pulses, and low-fat milk.
- Develop healthy eating habits, exercise regularly, and move as much as you can to avoid a sedentary lifestyle.

Guideline 2: Ensure the provision of extra food and healthcare for pregnant and lactating women.

Rationale

- Pregnancy is physiologically and nutritionally a highly demanding period. Extra food is required to meet the requirements of the foetus.
- The mother prepares herself to meet the nutritional demands by increasing her own body fat deposits during pregnancy.
- A lactating mother requires extra food to secrete adequate quantity and quality of milk and to safeguard her own health.

Points to Keep in Mind

- Eat more food during pregnancy.
- Eat more whole grains, sprouted grams, and fermented foods.
- Take milk/meat/eggs in adequate amounts.
- Eat plenty of vegetables and fruits.
- Avoid superstitions and food taboos.
- Do not use alcohol and tobacco. Also, take medicines only when prescribed.
- Take iron, folate, and calcium supplements regularly, after 14-16 weeks of pregnancy and continue the same during lactation.

Guideline 3: Promote exclusive breastfeeding for six months and encourage breastfeeding for first two years or more, if possible.

Rationale

Exclusive breastfeeding ensures safe nutrition for infants and helps in the all-round development of health.

- Breast milk is the most natural and ideal food for normal growth and healthy development of infants.
- Colostrum is rich in nutrients and anti-infective factors and should be fed to infants.
- Breastfeeding reduces the risk of infections.
- It establishes mother-infant contact and promotes mother-child bonding.
- It prolongs birth interval by fertility control (delayed return of menstruation).
- Breastfeeding helps in retraction of the uterus.

- The incidence of breast cancer is lower in mothers who breastfeed their children.
- Breastfeeding is associated with better cognitive development in children and may provide some long-term health benefits as well.

Points to Keep in Mind

- Start breastfeeding within an hour after delivery and do not discard colostrum.
- Breastfeed exclusively (not even water should be fed) for a minimum of six months, if the growth of the infant is adequate.
- Continue breastfeeding in addition to nutrient-rich complementary foods (weaning foods), preferably up to 2 years.
- Breastfeed the infant frequently and on-demand to establish and maintain a good milk supply.
- Take a nutritionally adequate diet both during pregnancy and lactation.
- Avoid tobacco (smoking and chewing), alcohol, and drugs during lactation.
- Ensure active family support for breastfeeding.

Guideline 4: Feed homemade semi-solid foods to the infants after six months.

Rationale

Easy-to-cook homemade preparations are hygienic and healthy foods for the growing baby.

- Breast milk alone is not adequate for an infant beyond 6 months of age.
- The introduction of food supplements (semi-solid

complementary foods) along with breastfeeding is necessary for infants after 6 months of age.

- The provision of adequate and appropriate supplements for young children prevents malnutrition.
- Hygienic practices should be observed while preparing and feeding the complementary food to the child; otherwise, it will lead to diarrhoea.
- Adequate food supplements should be provided in addition to continued breastfeeding from the age of 6 months onwards.

Points to Keep in Mind

- Breast milk alone is not enough for infants after 6 months of age.
- Complementary foods should be given after 6 months of age, in addition to breastfeeding.
- Do not delay complementary feeding.
- Feed low-cost homemade complementary foods.
- Feed complementary food on demand, ideally 3-4 times a day.
- Provide fruits and well-cooked vegetables.
- Observe hygienic practices while preparing and feeding the complementary food.
- Read the nutrition labels on baby foods carefully.

What Should Be Done If Breast Milk Is Not Adequate?

- If breastfeeding fails, the infant needs to be fed animal milk or commercial infant formula.
- Milk should be boiled before being fed to the baby.
- To start with, milk may be diluted with an equal volume of water.

- Full-strength milk may be started from 4 weeks of age.
- Infants fed animal milk should receive supplements of iron and vitamin C.
- About 120-180 ml of milk should be fed with one teaspoon of sugar per feed, 6-8 times over the day.
- While reconstituting the infant formula, the instructions given on the label should be strictly followed.
- The feeds should be prepared and given using a sterile cup, spoon, bottles, and nipples.
- Overfeeding should be avoided in artificially-fed infants to prevent obesity.
- Low-cost homemade complementary foods should be preferred.

Guideline 5: Ensure adequate and appropriate diets for children and adolescents, both in health and sickness.

Rationale

Well-formulated balanced diets for children and adolescents help in optimum growth and boost immunity.

- A nutritionally adequate and balanced diet is essential for optimal growth and development.
- Appropriate diet and physical activity during childhood are essential for optimum body composition and BMI and to reduce the risk of diet-related chronic diseases in later life and prevent vitamin deficiency.
- Common infections and malnutrition contribute significantly to child morbidity and mortality.

- A child needs to eat more during and after episodes of infections to maintain good nutritional status.

Points to Keep in Mind

- Take extra care in feeding a young child and include soft-cooked vegetables and seasonal fruits.
- Give plenty of milk and milk products to children and adolescents.
- Promote physical activity and appropriate lifestyle practices.
- Discourage overeating as well as indiscriminate dieting.

Points to Keep in Mind During Illness

- Never starve the child.
- Feed energy-rich cereals-pulse diet with milk and mashed vegetables.
- Feed small quantities at frequent intervals.
- Continue breastfeeding as long as possible.
- Give plenty of fluids during illness.
- Use oral rehydration solution to prevent and correct dehydration during diarrhoea episodes.

Guideline 6: Eat plenty of vegetables and fruits.

Rationale

Green leafy vegetables, other vegetables, and fresh fruits are a treasure trove of several minerals, vitamins and iron, and hence, protect from diseases.

- For a normal diet to be wholesome and tasty, fresh vegetables and fruit should be included, which are storehouses of micronutrients.

- Vegetables and fruits are rich sources of micronutrients.
- Fruits and vegetables also provide phytonutrients and fibre which are of vital health significance.
- They help in the prevention of micronutrient malnutrition and certain chronic diseases such as cardiovascular diseases, cataracts, and cancer.
- Fresh fruits are nutritionally superior to fruit juices.

Points to Keep in Mind

- Include green leafy vegetables in your daily diet.
- Eat as much vegetables as possible daily.
- Eat vegetables and fruits with all your meals in various forms (curry, soups, mixed with curd, added to pulse preparations and rice, etc.).
- Consume raw and fresh vegetables as salads.
- Grow the family's requirements of vegetables in the kitchen garden if possible.
- Green leafy vegetables, when properly cleaned and cooked, are safe even for infants.
- Let different varieties of vegetables and fruits add colour to your plate and vitality to your life.
- Beta-carotene-rich foods like dark green, yellow, and orange coloured vegetables and fruits (GLVs, carrots, papaya, and mangoes) protect from vitamin A deficiency.

Guideline 7: Ensure moderate use of edible oils and animal foods and very little use of ghee/ butter/ vanaspati.

Rationale

Excessive use of plant and animal-based fats causes elevation of blood lipids, thereby leading to increased risk of heart diseases and other illnesses.

- Fats/oils have high energy value and induce satiety.
- Fats provide energy and essential fatty acids and promote absorption of fat-soluble vitamins.
- Fats are precursors of biologically active compounds in the body.
- Diets that provide excess of calories, fats, and cholesterol elevate blood lipids (cholesterol and triglycerides) and promote blood clotting.
- Excessive fat in the diet increases the risk of obesity, heart disease, stroke, and cancer.
- The ill effects of excess dietary fats are initiated early in life.

Points to Keep in Mind

- Keep fat intake in moderation.
- Substitute part of visible fat and invisible fat from animal foods with whole nuts.
- Moderate the use of animal foods containing high fat, SFA, and cholesterol.
- Limit the use of ghee, butter, and especially vanaspati, as a cooking oil.
- Choose low-fat dairy foods in place of regular whole-fat dairy foods.
- Eat foods rich in alpha-linolenic (ALA) acid such

as legumes, green leafy vegetables, fenugreek, and mustard seeds.

- Eat fish more frequently (at least 100-200g/week), prefer it over meat and poultry, and limit/avoid organ meats such as liver, kidney, brain, etc.
- Egg has several important nutrients but is high in cholesterol. Limit the consumption to 3 eggs/week. However, egg whites may be consumed in good amounts.
- Minimise consumption of ready-to-eat fast foods, bakery foods, and processed foods prepared in hydrogenated fat.
- Reheated fats and oils should be avoided.
- Use fats and oils in moderation and consume a variety of foods to get a good proportion of all fatty acids for optimal health benefits.

Guideline 8: Avoid overeating to prevent overweight and obesity.

Rationale

Overweight/obesity is the causative factor for several chronic non-communicable diseases including heart disease, diabetes, and certain types of cancers.

- A dramatic increase in the prevalence of overweight and obesity among all age groups has occurred in the last 2-3 decades.
- About 30-50 per cent of adult Indians are either overweight or obese.
- Overweight and obese individuals are at a higher risk of comorbidities including type 2 diabetes, fatty liver disease, gallstones, high blood cholesterol and

triglycerides, orthopaedic disorders (osteoarthritis), hypertension, cardiovascular diseases, certain cancers, and psycho-social problems.
- The imbalance between energy intake and energy output leads to excess accumulation of fat in various parts of the body.

Points to Keep in Mind

- A slow and steady reduction in body weight is advisable.
- Severe fasting may lead to health hazards.
- Achieve energy balance and appropriate weight for height.
- Encourage regular physical activity.
- Eat small meals regularly at frequent intervals.
- Cut down on sugar, salt, fatty foods, refined foods, soft drinks, and alcohol.
- Eat complex carbohydrates, low glycaemic foods, and fibre-rich diets.
- Increase consumption of fruits, vegetables, legumes, whole grains, and nuts.
- Limit fat intake and shift from saturated to unsaturated fats.
- Avoid trans-fatty rich foods (vanaspati, bakery products and sweets).
- Use low-fat milk.

Guideline 9: Exercise regularly and be physically active to maintain an ideal body weight.

Rationale

Regular physical exercise increases strength and stamina, elevates 'good' cholesterol, and improves overall health.

- Physical activity of moderate intensity is recommended for health and well-being.
- Physical activity is essential to maintain ideal body weight by burning excess calories and for the prevention of non-communicable diseases.
- Physical activity is a major modifiable factor in the reduction of non-communicable chronic diseases.
- Physical activity may reduce the risk of falls and injuries in the elderly.
- Exercise is a prescriptive medicine.
- Move your body as much as you can.

Points to Keep in Mind

- A minimum of 30-45 minutes of brisk walking or any physical activity of moderate intensity improves overall health.
- Include warm-up and cool-down periods before and after the exercise regimen.
- 45 minutes per day of moderate-intensity physical activity provides many health benefits.

Guideline 10: Restrict salt intake to a minimum.

Rationale

Increased salt intake can pose a health risk and may lead to hypertension and heart disease.

- Sodium plays an important role in nerve conduction and fluid balance in the body.
- Maintenance of sodium balance depends on kidney function.
- High intake of salt (sodium chloride) is associated with high blood pressure and stomach cancer.
- All foods contain sodium. Sodium requirements can be met with moderate salt intake.
- Sodium intake needs to be balanced by potassium intake.

Points to Keep in Mind

- Restrict the intake of added salt right from an early age.
- Develop a taste for foods/diets that are low in salt.
- Restrict intake of preserved and processed foods such as papads, pickles, sauces, ketchup, salted biscuits, chips, cheese, and salted fish.
- Eat plenty of vegetables and fruits as they are good sources of potassium.
- Always use iron-fortified iodised salt (double-fortified salt).

Guideline 11: Ensure the use of safe and clean foods.

Rationale

Contaminated and adulterated foods are major causes of several food-borne illnesses in the country.

- Safe and good quality foods are essential for maintaining good health.
- Naturally occurring toxins, environmental contaminants, and adulterants in foods constitute a health hazard.
- Consumption of unsafe foods can lead to food-borne diseases.

Guideline 12: Adopt the right pre-cooking processes and appropriate cooking methods.

Rationale

Healthy and positive food concepts and cooking practices are the foundation of good health.

- Cultural factors play an important role in dietary practices.
- Faulty food fads and beliefs adversely affect nutrition and health.
- Cooking renders food palatable and helps in easy digestion.
- Cooking destroys harmful germs.
- Faulty pre-cooking and cooking processes lead to loss of nutrients.
- Cooking at high temperatures leads to the

destruction of nutrients and the formation of harmful substances.

Points to Keep in Mind

- Do not wash food grains repeatedly before cooking.
- Do not wash vegetables after cutting.
- Do not soak the cut vegetables in water for long periods.
- Do not discard the excess water left over after cooking. Use only sufficient water for cooking.
- Cook foods in vessels covered with lids.
- Prefer pressure/steam cooking to deep frying/ roasting.
- Encourage consumption of sprouted/fermented foods.
- Avoid the use of baking soda while cooking pulses and vegetables.
- Do not reheat the leftover oil repeatedly.
- Avoid food fads and discard erroneous food beliefs.

Guideline 13: Drink plenty of water and take beverages in moderation.

Rationale

Water is the most important nutrient of all, and it helps in the upkeep of our health.

- Water is the major constituent of the human body.
- Beverages are useful to relieve thirst and to meet the fluid requirements of the body.

- Some beverages provide nutrients while others act as stimulants.
- Milk is an excellent beverage for all age groups as it is a rich source of nutrients.

Points to Keep in Mind

- Drink enough safe and quality water to meet daily fluid requirements.
- Drink boiled water when the safety of the water is in doubt.
- Consume at least 250 ml of boiled or pasteurised milk per day.
- Drink natural and fresh fruit juices instead of carbonated beverages.
- Prefer tea over coffee.
- Avoid alcohol, and those who drink should limit its intake.

Guideline 14: Minimise the use of processed foods rich in salt, sugar, and fats.

Rationale

Processed foods being rich in fats, salt, sugar, and preservatives may pose a health risk, if consumed regularly.

- Urbanisation has increased the intake and demand for processed foods.
- There is a trend towards replacing traditionally cooked foods with processed foods.

- Processed foods may not be nutritionally balanced unless fortified.
- Sugar, a processed food, provides empty calories.

Points to Keep in Mind

- Prefer traditional, homemade foods.
- Avoid replacing meals with snack foods.
- Limit consumption of sugar and unhealthy processed foods which provide only (empty) calories.
- Prefer fortified processed foods.
- Always read food labels (given on containers) regarding the content of nutrients, shelf-life, and the additives present.

Guideline 15: Include micronutrient-rich foods in the diets of elderly people to enable them to be fit and active.

Rationale

Senior citizens need more vitamins and minerals to remain healthy and active.

- Body composition changes with advancing age, and these changes affect the nutritional needs of elderly people.
- Elderly or aged people require reduced amounts of calories, as their lean muscle mass and physical activity decrease with age.
- Elderly people are more prone to diseases due to lowered food intake, physical activity, and resistance to infection.

- Good/healthy food habits and a regular comfortable level of physical activity are required to minimise the ill effects of ageing and to improve the quality of life.
- Elderly people need adequate amounts of protein, carbohydrates, fat, vitamins, minerals, and dietary fibre.
- Elderly people need more calcium, iron, zinc, vitamin A, and antioxidants to prevent age-related degenerative diseases and for healthy ageing.

Points to Keep in Mind

- Eat a variety of nutrient-rich foods.
- Match food intake with physical activity.
- Eat food in many divided portions in a day.
- Avoid fried, salty, and spicy foods.
- Consume adequate water to avoid dehydration.
- Exercise regularly.

Salient Points

- The food we eat must be scrutinised carefully and our meals should be appropriate for our age, sex, and physical status.
- Emphasis on locally available foods should be given.
- Exercise is essential for good health.
- Promote exclusive breastfeeding for 6 months and it should be continued along with complementary feeds till 2 years of age.
- Locally available sourced foods must be encouraged for home-based semi-solid complementary feeds beyond 6 months of age.
- A well-balanced diet for children and adolescents is important both in health and sickness.
- Ensure balanced use of oils in daily cooking with restrained use of dalda.
- Encourage avoidance of junk and coloured food to prevent obesity.
- Avoid excessive salt intake.
- Promote proper cooking techniques to minimise loss of nutrients during the cooking process.
- Inculcate more water intake as water is the most important nutrient for the human body.

Epilogue

After having read the book completely and hopefully finding thought-provoking and insightful information, the reader needs to come to the hard task of implementing the various recommendations. It is much easier to learn something new than to unlearn certain beliefs and knowledge acquired over a long period of time.

The increase in food allergies is itself due to the paradigm and tectonic shift in our habits acquired over centuries. We live in a society where norms are not dictated by what is good and healthy but by what we see in our environment which is driven much by the media. And the media itself is driven by the powerful food and beverage corporations whose only concern is profits.

But even though it may be difficult to completely revert back to older ways as far as our food habits are concerned, we can always take the necessary steps discussed in this book to achieve optimal and holistic health. People in India have been blessed with a long-standing tradition of practices developed over centuries and many of them have protected us from lifestyle diseases including allergies. Thus, it is of crucial importance to strike a balance between what is normative in this fast-paced life and our traditional values. And if we are able to do so, we might succeed in slowing down the oncoming epidemic of food and skin allergies.

ACKNOWLEDGEMENTS

This book is a sequel to my earlier book, *Winning Over Allergies: Myths and Facts,* published by Hay House India. This book was done with much cooperation and contributions from many eminent personalities.

Foremost, I would like to thank my co-author, Dr. Sowmya Nagarajan. She is a young dynamic allergist and has provided invaluable feedback and fresh perspectives on many challenging and controversial ideas in the field of allergy.

I would also like to express my gratitude to Dr Professor Rekha Harish, ex-HOD, GMC, Jammu, also the Chairperson, NCD Prevention (IAP). Her article and research work were elucidating and helpful for the chapter on junk foods.

To Dr Geeta Patil, a senior consultant paediatrician in Bangalore, whose inspiring lecture on food colourants was the basis for highlighting the harmful effects of colourants in food.

To Dr Arakita Swain, professor in paediatrics, IMS and SUM Hospital, Bhubaneswar, who gave edifying insights into the traditional weaning practices across India.

To Jyotsana Kumari, a chef, food blogger, and cake artist, whose inputs were instrumental in writing the chapter on savoury recipes for weaning diet.

To Dr Ashraq my student, who helped with designing elements in this book.

To Dr Hemlatha, director at the National Institute of Nutrition, Hyderabad, who was kind enough to permit us to reproduce the institution's guidelines.

Finally, I am deeply indebted to my professor and mentor in allergy, Dr Peter Arkwright, from Royal Manchester Children's Hospital, who allowed us to print the information for parents published by the NHS North Western England authority.

About the Authors

Arif Ahmed

Arif Ahmed is an allergist and a paediatrician educated in India, the UK, and the USA. He graduated in medicine from the Seth GS Medical College in Mumbai and then pursued his post-graduation in paediatrics from the same reputed institute. In the United Kingdom, he worked as a senior resident in paediatrics and neonatology at the NHS hospitals for three years. He was a senior resident in paediatrics at the Sparrow Hospital and Michigan State University of Lansing, MI, USA.

He is now on the faculty board at Shadan Medical College as a professor and head of the department of paediatrics in addition to holding the post of senior consultant paediatrics at numerous teaching hospitals in Hyderabad. He is also the director and allergist at Allermy Centre for Allergy and Chest Diseases.

Dr Arif's interest was drawn towards allergy on account of witnessing the manifestation of allergies in individuals of the paediatric age group, which were left unattended or worse, brushed under the carpet of sinusitis or common cold, and this led to such issues snowballing into full-blown problems in adulthood.

He did a clinical attachment in allergy and immunology at The Royal Manchester Children's Hospital and has passed the European Board for Allergy and Immunology examination conducted by the European Academy of Allergy and Clinical Immunology in 2013 (first from

India). He has done extensive research work in allergy and immunology and presented numerous publications (national and international) that include books, papers, lectures, conferences, and workshops all over India besides oral and poster presentations in UAE, USA, and Europe. Over 200 lectures and workshops on allergy have been conducted by him in nooks and crannies across India to raise awareness amongst doctors. He has given numerous guest lectures throughout India including Dr Gaya Prasad Memorial in Patna and Dr Harish Chandra Memorial in Hyderabad.

He also conducts free camps for education, awareness, early detection, and treatment in the slums of Hyderabad and is a founding trustee and manager of the NGO SOWED (Specialist on Wheels for the Economically Deprived). He is the author of *Winning over Allergies: Myths and Facts* published by Hay House India. He has a YouTube channel 'Dr Arif Ahmed Allermy' and a website (www.allermy.com) for educating public about allergic diseases.

He is available on e-mail: arifahmed1960@gmail.com.

Sowmya Nagarajan

Sowmya Nagarajan is a paediatrician, allergist, and immunologist trained in India, Singapore, and the United Kingdom. She graduated in medicine from Sri Siddhartha Medical College in Tumkur, Karnataka, and then pursued her post-graduation in paediatrics from M. S. Ramaiah Medical College, Bengaluru. She has worked in Manipal Hospitals, Bengaluru, as a senior resident.

Her interest in allergies and immunology was sparked by her desire to do more for her patients. Pursuing her interest in allergy and immunology, she worked as a clinical fellow at the prestigious National University Hospitals, Singapore. She has also completed a diploma in allergy and asthma from the reputed Christian Medical College, Vellore, India. She was in St. James Hospital, Leeds, UK, as a part of J. M. grant from the European Academy of Allergy and Clinical Immunology. She is also a diplomate in the methodology of systematic reviews and meta-analysis (John Hopkins College, USA) and is one of the few board-certified specialists in allergy and immunology from the European Academy of Allergy and Clinical Immunology.

Presently, she is a consultant paediatrician, allergist, and immunologist, practicing at Sanjeevini Specialist Clinic, Motherhood hospitals, and Allergy Central in Bengaluru and also a reviewer for the journal, *Allergy*. She conducts regular camps for patient treatment, education, and support groups in rural parts of Karnataka.

She can be contacted on her email: dr.sowmya.nagaraj@gmail.com.

Bibliography

Section I

Chapter 2: The Burden of Food Allergy

1. National Academies of Sciences, Engineering, and Medicine; Health and Medicine Division; Food and Nutrition Board; Committee on Food Allergies: Global Burden, Causes, Treatment, Prevention, and Public Policy; Oria MP, Stallings VA, editors. Finding a Path to Safety in Food Allergy: Assessment of the Global Burden, Causes, Prevention, Management, and Public Policy. Washington (DC): National Academies Press (US); 2016 Nov 30. 3, Prevalence. Link: https://www.ncbi.nlm.nih.gov/books/NBK435940.
2. Loh, W., Tang, M.L.K., The Epidemiology of Food Allergy in the Global Context. *Int. J. Environ. Res. Public Health,* 2018, *15,* 2043. Link: https://doi.org/10.3390/ijerph15092043.
3. Mahesh P. A., Wong, G. W., Ogorodova, L., Potts, J., Leung, T. F., Fedorova O., Holla A.D., Fernandez-Rivas, M., Clare Mills, E.N., Kummeling, I., et al. Prevalence of food sensitisation and probable food allergy among adults in India. The EuroPrevall INCO study, Allergy, 2016, 71, 1010-1019.

Chapter 3: Hygiene Hypothesis

1. Bloomfield S.F., Stanwell-Smith R., Crevel R.W., Pickup J., Too clean, or not too clean: the hygiene

hypothesis and home hygiene. Clin Exp Allergy, April 2006, 36(4):402-25, DOI: 10.1111/j.1365-2222.2006.02463.x. PMID: 16630145, PMCID: PMC1448690.

2. Thomsen S.F., Epidemiology and natural history of atopic diseases, Eur Clin Respir J. 2015 Mar 24;2, DOI: 10.3402/ecrj.v2.24642. PMID: 26557262, PMCID: PMC4629767.
3. Herbert O.Ch., Barnetson R.S., Weninger W., Krämer U., Behrendt H., Ring J., Western lifestyle and increased prevalence of atopic diseases: an example from a small Papua New Guinean Island, World Allergy Organ J., July 2009 Jul, 2(7):130-7, DOI: 10.1097/WOX.0b013e3181accf27, PMID: 23283062, PMCID: PMC3650959.
4. Centers for Disease Control and Prevention. (2019), *FastStats: Allergies and Hay Fever,* U.S. Department of Health and Human Services. Link: https://www.cdc.gov/nchs/fastats/allergies.htm.
5. Gupta R.S., Warren C.M., Smith B.M., Jiang, J., Blumenstock, J.A., Davis, M.M., Schleimer R.P., and Nadeau K.C. (2019), Prevalence and Severity of Food Allergies Among US Adults, *JAMA Network Open*, *2*(1), e185630. Link: https://doi.org/10.1001/jamanetworkopen.2018.5630.
6. Gupta, R.S., Warren C.M., Smith B.M., Blumenstock J.A., Jiang J., Davis M.M., and Nadeau K.C. (2018), The Public Health Impact of Parent-Reported Childhood Food Allergies in the United States, *Pediatrics*, *142*(6). Link: https://doi.org/10.1542/peds.2018-1235.

Section II

Chapter 1: The Body's Defence Mechanism

1. Kaiser GE, The Innate Immune System. Dr Kaiser's Microbiology home page, Community College Baltimore County, 2007 [cited 31 January 2012]. Link: http://faculty.ccbcmd.edu/~gkaiser/welcome.html.
2. Marieb Elaine, Essential of Human Anatomy and Physiology, 7th edition, San Francisco, Benjamin Cummings, 2003.
3. Baroody F.M., Naclerio R.M., World Allergy Org J. 2011; 4(1), S1-5.
4. Peakman M. and Vergani D., Basic and Clinical Immunology, 1997, Churchill Livingstone, New York.
5. Ghaffar A., Hypersensitivity Reactions, chapter 17, Microbiology and Immunology, University of South Carolina, 2010 [cited 26 January 2012].

Chapter 3: IgE Mediated Food Allergy

1. Sicherer S.H., Wood R.A., Vickery B.P., Jones S.M., Liu A.H., Fleischer D.M., et al, The natural history of egg allergy in an observational cohort, J Allergy Clin Immunol (2014), 133:1041, 10.1016/j.jaci.2013.12.104.
2. Savage J.H., Matsui E.C., Skripak J.M., Wood R.A., The natural history of egg allergy, J Allergy Clin Immunol (2007), 120:1413-7, 10.1016/j.jaci.2007.09.040.
3. Caubet J.C., Lin J., Ahrens B., Gimenez G., Bardina L., Niggemann B., Sampson H.A., Beyer K., Natural tolerance development in cow's milk allergic children: IgE and IgG4 epitope binding, Allergy, November

2017, 72(11):1677-1685, DOI: 10.1111/all.13167, Epub 2017 June 9, PMID: 28345783.

4. Pantipa Chatchatee, Anna Nowak-Wegrzyn, Lars Lange, Suwat Benjaponpitak, Kok Wee Chong, Pasuree Sangsupawanich, Marleen T.J. van Ampting, Manon M. Oude Nijhuis, Lucien F. Harthoorn, Jane E. Langford, Jan Knol, Karen Knipping, Johan Garssen, Valerie Trendelenburg, Robert Pesek, Carla M. Davis, Antonella Muraro, MichErlewyn-Lajeunesse, Adam T. Fox, Louise J. Michaelis, Kirsten Beyer, Lee Noimark, Gary Stiefel, Uwe Schauer, undefined Hamelman, Diego Peroni, undefined Boner, Tolerance development in cow's milk-allergic infants receiving amino acid-based formula, A randomised controlled trial, Journal of Allergy and Clinical Immunology, 10.1016/j.jaci.2021.06.025, 149, 2, (650-658.e5), (2022).
5. Survey data to guide diagnostic testing for Paediatric Food Allergy and Anaphylaxis prevention in India, Ryan Din, Sowmya Nagarajan, et al, poster presentation in APAPARI 2021
6. Sussman G., Sussman A., Sussman D., Oral allergy syndrome, CMAJ, 2010 Aug 10, 182(11):1210-1, DOI: 10.1503/cmaj.090314, Epub 2010 Jun 21, PMID: 20566728, PMCID: PMC2917934.
7. Uft L, Blumstein G.I., Studies in food allergy: II, Sensitisation to fresh fruits: clinical and experimental observations, J Allergy, 1942;13(6):574-82.
8. Mari A., Ballmer-Weber B.K., Vieths S., The oral allergy syndrome: improved diagnostic and treatment methods, CurrOpin Allergy Clin Immunol, 2005;5(3):267-73.

9. Tuano K., Davis C., Oral allergy syndrome in shrimp and house dust mite allergies, J Allergy Clin Immunol Pract, 2018;6(6):2163-4.

Chapter 4: Non-IgE Mediated Food Allergy

1. https://www.aaaai.org/conditions-treatments/related-conditions/eosinophilic-esophagitis.
2. Gonsalves N.P., Aceves S.S., Diagnosis and treatment of eosinophilic esophagitis, J Allergy Clin Immunol, 2020 Jan, 145(1):1-7, DOI: 10.1016/j.jaci.2019.11.011, PMID: 31910983, PMCID: PMC6986782.5.

Chapter 5: Systemic Manifestations of Food Allergies

1. Wüthrich B., Food-induced cutaneous adverse reactions, Allergy, 1998;53(46 Suppl):131-5, DOI: 10.1111/j.1398-9995.1998.tb04983.x, PMID: 9826020.
2. Zukiewicz-Sobczak W.A., Wróblewska P., Adamczuk P., Kopczyński P., Causes, symptoms, and prevention of food allergy, Postepy Dermatol Alergol, 2013 Apr;30(2):113-6, DOI: 10.5114/pdia.2013.34162, Epub 2013 Apr 12, PMID: 24278058, PMCID: PMC3834685.
3. https://doi.org/10.1067/mai.2000.110158.

Chapter 6: Acute and Life-Threatening Allergies—Anaphylaxis

1. National Institutes of Health. Link: https://www.niaid.nih.gov.

Section III

Chapter 1: Laboratory Diagnosis of Allergic Diseases

1. Mueller G.A., Maleki S.J., Pedersen L.C., The molecular basis of peanut allergy, Curr Allergy Asthma Rep, 2014 May;14(5):429, DOI: 10.1007/s11882-014-0429-5, PMID: 24633613, PMCID: PMC4785306.
2. Becker W.M., Petersen A., Jappe U., Peanut allergens: new consolidated findings on structure, characteristics, and allergome, Allergol Select, 2018 Sep 1;2(1):67-79, DOI: 10.5414/ALX01418E, PMID: 31826045, PMCID: PMC6881859.

Chapter 4: Oral Home Challenge

1. https://doi.org/10.1016/j.jaip.2022.09.040.
2. https://doi.org/10.1016/j.jaip.2022.09.040.

Section V

Chapter 1: Diagnosis of Common Food Allergens

1. https://allergynorthwest.nhs.uk/resources/allergy-leaflets/home-milk-challenge.

Chapter 3: Food Additives, Preservatives, and Colourants

1. Trasande L., Shaffer R.M., Sathyanarayana S., Council on Environmental Health, Food Additives and Child Health, Pediatrics, 2018 Aug;142(2):e20181410, DOI:10.1542/peds.2018-1410, PMID: 30037972, PMCID: PMC6298598.
2. Chazelas, E., Druesne-Pecollo N., Esseddik Y., et al. Exposure to food additive mixtures in 106,000 French

adults from the NutriNet-Santé cohort, Sci Rep11, 19680 (2021), https://doi.org/10.1038/s41598-021-98496-6.

3. Trasnade L., Shaffer R.M., Sathyanarayana S., American Academy of Pediatrics Council on Environmental Health, Technical report food additives and child health, Paediatrics 2018: 142(2): e20181408 (PMC free article) (Pub Med) (Google Scholar).
4. K.E. Elizabeth, Nutrition and Child Development, 6th edition, Applied Nutrition, Free radicals, Antioxidants, Phytochemical, page 276, Bhat, Rajeev: Alias, Abd Karim Paliyath, Gopinadham (2011), Progress in Food Preservation. Link: http://www.eblib.com.
5. Food Standards Agency, Fed Regist. 1, Codified as 21 CFR 70 [Google Scholarvens L.J., Burgess J.R., Stochelski M.A., Kuczek T., Amounts of artificial food colours in commonly consumed beverages and potential behavioural implications for consumption in children, Clin Pediatr (Phila), 2014;53(2):133-140 [PubMed].
6. Health line, Is MSG truly unhealthy? All you need to know, Ariane Lang, Medically reviewed by Maya Feller Nutrition updated on November 15, 2021.
7. Flavouring and Colouring Agents: Health Risks and Potential Problems January 2018, DOI:10.1016/B978-0-12-811518-3.00001-6, Natural and Artificial Flavouring Agents and Food Dyes (pp.1-28), Muthuswamy Ramesh, Arunachalam Muthuraman, JSS Medical college, Mysuru.
8. K.E. Elizabeth, Nutrition and Child Development, Free radicals, Antioxidants, Phytochemicals, Zero Calorie, and Empty Calorie Foods, Page 283.

9. Occupational pesticide exposure and symptoms of ADHD in adolescent pesticide applicators in Egypt, Diane S. Rohlman, Ahemad Ismail, Mathew R. Bonner, Gafar Abdul Rasoul, Olfat Handy, Lizette Ortega Dickey, Kai Wang, James R. Olson, PMID: 31077682 PMCID: PMC 6751012 DOI:10.1016/ J neuro2019.05.002 11, published online in the journal Environmental Health, 3 June 2015.

Appendix I

Chapter 1: Breastfeeding

1. Infant and young child feeding, World Health Organization, 9 June 2021. Link: https://www.who.int › Newsroom › Fact sheets › Detail.
2. The association of prolonged breastfeeding and allergic disease in poor urban children C, C. Obihara, B.J. Marais, R.P. Gie, P. Potter, E.D. Bateman, C.J. Lombard, N. Beyers, J.L.L. Kimpen, European Respiratory Journal, June 2005, 25 (6) 970-977, DOI: 10.1183/09031936.05.00116504.

Chapter 2: Traditional Indian Weaning Diets

1. LEAP study results: Randomised Trial of Peanut Consumption in Infants at Risk for Peanut Allergy

2. George Du Toit, M.B., B.Ch., Graham Roberts, D. M., Peter H. Sayre, M.D., Ph.D., Henry T. Bahnson, M.P.H., Suzana Radulovic, M.D., Alexandra F. Santos, M.D., Helen A. Brough, M.B., B.S., Deborah Phippard, Ph.D., Monica Basting, M.A., Mary Feeney, M.Sc., R.D., Victor Turcanu, M.D., Ph.D., Michelle L. Sever, M.S.P.H., Ph.D.et al for the LEAP Study Team

February 26, 2015 N Engl J Med 2015; 372:803-813 DOI: 10.1056/NEJMoa1414850.

Appendix II

Chapter 1: JUNCS Food

1. Draft guidelines for regulating food high in fat, sugar, and salt (HFSS) also popularly known as junk food. Link: www.indiaenvironmentportal.org.in/.../Junk per cent20Food per cent20Guidelines per cent20- per cent20January.
2. Jacka F.N., Mykletun A., Berk M., Bjelland I., Tell G.S., The association between habitual diet quality and the common mental disorders in community-dwelling adults: The Hordaland Health Study, Psychosom Med. 2011, 73:483-90.
3. World Health Organization, Guideline: Sugars Intake for Adults and Children, Geneva, World Health Organization, 2015.
4. US Department of Health and Human Services and US Department of Agriculture, 2015-2020, Dietary Guidelines for Americans, 8th ed., December 2015. Link: http://health.gov/dietaryguidelines/2015/guidelines/.
5. Scientific Advisory Committee on Nutrition (2015), Carbohydrates and Health. Link: https://www.gov.uk/government/uploads/system/uploads/attachment_data/file/445503/SACN_Carbohydrates_and_Health.pdf.
6. Fidler Mis N., Braegger C., Bronsky J., Campoy C., Domellöf M., Embleton N.D., et al. ESPGHAN Committee on Nutrition. Sugar in Infants, Children, and Adolescents: A position paper of the European

Society for Paediatric Gastroenterology, Hepatology, and Nutrition Committee on Nutrition. J Pediatr Gastroenterol Nutr., 2017;65:681-96.
7. World Health Organization, Healthy Diet. Link: https://www.who.int/news-room/factsheets/detail/healthy-diet.
8. World Health Organization, Guideline: Sodium Intake for Adults and Children. Geneva, WHO, 2012.
9. World Health Organization (WHO), 2008-2013 Action Plan for the Global Strategy for the Prevention and Control of Non-Communicable Diseases, Geneva, WHO, 2008.
10. Bergallo P., Castagnari V., Fernández A., Mejía R., Regulatory initiatives to reduce sugar-sweetened beverages (SSBs) in Latin America, PLoS One, 2018;13:e0205694.
11. *The Times of India,* Time up for junk food in school canteens in Delhi. Link: https://timesofindia.indiatimes.com/city/delhi/Time-up-for-junk-food-in-school-canteens-in-Delhi/articleshow/49422275.cms.
12. Heyman M.B., Abrams S.A., AAP Section on Gastroenterology, Hepatology, and Nutrition, AAP Committee on Nutrition, Fruit Juice in Infants, Children, and Adolescents, Current Recommendations, Pediatrics, 2017;139:e20170967.
13. World Health Organization, Global Recommendations on Physical Activity for Health, Geneva, World Health Organization, 2010.
14. Foodnavigator-asia.com, APAC sugar taxes: How 2018 is shaping up from a policy perspective. Link: https://www.foodnavigator-asia.com/Article/2018/01/03/APAC-sugar-taxes-How-2018-is-shaping-up-from-a-policy-perspective.

15. American Academy of Pediatrics, 'Sports Drinks and Energy Drinks for Children and Adolescents: Are they appropriate?', Committee on Nutrition and the Council on Sports Medicine and Fitness, Pediatrics, 2011;127:1182-9.
16. American College of Sports Medicine Updated Energy Drink Guidelines, Summit Medical Group. Link: https://www.summitmedicalgroup.com/news/nutrition/american-collegesports-medicine-updated-energy-drink-guidelines/.
17. EFSA NDA Panel (EFSA Panel on Dietetic Products, Nutrition and Allergies), 2015, Scientific Opinion on the safety of caffeine, EFSA Journal, 2015;13:4102.
18. ICBA Guidelines for the Composition, Labelling, and Responsible Marketing of Energy Drinks. Link: http://www.icba-net.org/files/resources/energy-drink-guidelines.pdf.
19. UNESDA Code for the Labelling and Marketing of Energy Drinks, UNESDA—Soft Drinks Europe, Link: https://www.unesda.eu/wp-content/uploads/2018/02/Updated-UNESDAEnergy-Drinks-Code_November-2017.pdf.
20. American Beverage Association, ABA Guidance for the Responsible Labelling and Marketing of Energy Drinks, Link: https://www.ameribev.org/les/resources/2014-energy-drinksguidance-approved-by-bod-43020c.pdf.
21. Food Safety and Standards Authority of India, Food Safety and Standards Authority of India proposes regulation of energy drinks, and caffeine (Revised). Link: https://old.fssai.gov.in/Portals/0/standards_of_energy_drinks_.pdf.

Glossary

Atopic: It refers to the genetic make-up of the individual.

Anaphylaxis: A severe, life-threatening, generalised, or systemic hypersensitivity reaction.

Antigens: Molecules that stimulate antibody production.

Angioedema: Angioedema is an area of swelling of the deeper layers of skin and tissue, just under the skin or mucous membranes.

B lymphocytes: White blood cells, which function as antibodies.

Bilateral: Both sides (right and left).

Bronchodilators: Drugs that open up the respiratory passages in asthma.

Catalyse: To speed up a process, especially a chemical or biochemical reaction.

Chemokines: Molecules that induce movement in certain cells.

Cytokines: Molecules that have an effect on the behaviour of certain cells.

Chronic: Long-standing (minimum 6 weeks duration).

Chelates: Class of coordination or complex compounds consisting of a central metal atom attached to a large molecule, called a ligand.

Cognitive: Relating to, being, or involving conscious intellectual activity like thinking.

Corneal: The glass-like structure covering the eyes.

Cyanosis: Bluish discolouration of lips, tongue, and nails.

Cysteinyl Leukotrienes: Cysteine (an amino acid) containing leukotriene (molecules originally isolated from leucocytes and are metabolites of arachidonic acid, containing three conjugated double bonds).

Degranulation: Process that releases granules (which may contain antimicrobial cytotoxic or other molecules) found inside the cells.

Drug Tolerance: Reduced reaction to a drug following its repeated use.

Dysbiosis: An imbalance in the gut microbial community that is associated with disease.

Dyslipidaemia: An abnormal amount of lipids (e.g., triglycerides, cholesterol, and/or fat phospholipids) in the blood.

Oedema: Swelling of the inner lining of the organs.

Eosinophils: White blood cells that have granules easily stained by eosin.

Epidermis: The most superficial layer of the skin, lying over the dermis.

Eustachian tube: A tube connecting the nose to the ears.

Epitopes: The part of an antigen or allergen molecule to which an antibody attaches itself.

Fungi: Microscopic growth of moulds found on rotting food or damp areas.

Gut Microbiome: The microbiome consists of microbes that are both helpful and potentially harmful.

Haptenation: Reaction or coordination with a hapten.

Histamine: Histamine is a protein molecule with the chemical formula C5H9N3, that mediates local immune responses and physiological function in the gut and also acts as a neurotransmitter.

Hydrocolloid: A substance that forms a gel in the presence of water, examples of which are used in surgical dressings and in various industrial applications.

Hygroscopic: Tending to absorb moisture from the air.

Hypoxia: Condition in which tissues are deprived of oxygen.

Idiopathic: Disease for which the cause is unknown.

Immunological: To do with the immune system.

Immiscible: Not forming a homogeneous mixture when mixed.

Intradermal: Within the skin.

Inflammatory: To do with inflammation (the body's natural response to an external or rarely, an internal stimulus, resulting in swelling, redness, and pain).

Inoculate: Introduce (cells or organisms) into a culture medium.

In Vitro: Performed or taking place outside a living organism (especially, in a test tube or culture dish).

In Vivo: Performed or taking place in a living organism.

Innate immunity: First response of the body's immune system to a harmful foreign substance.

Lymphatic: To do with lymph (a colourless fluid with white blood cells, that bathes the tissues and drains through the lymphatic system into the bloodstream).

Leukotrienes: Molecules originally isolated from leucocytes and are metabolites of arachidonic acid, containing three conjugated double bonds.

Laryngospasm: Contracture of respiratory muscles which may happen during an allergic reaction, which may cause difficulty in breathing.

Mast Cells: WBC with granules containing histamine, heparin, and a non-lobulated round nucleus (present in tissues and outside blood).

Metabolic Dysregulation: A metabolic disorder occurs when the metabolism process fails and causes the body to have either too much or too little of the essential substances needed to stay healthy.

Microscopic: Not visible to the naked eye.

Microbes: Microbes are small living things that are present in our environment and are too small to be seen by the naked eye and can be appreciated better under the microscope.

Molecules: The smallest particle of a substance that has all of the physical and chemical properties of that substance.

Mucosa: Mucosa is moist tissue that lines certain parts of the inside of your body. It is present in the nose, mouth, lungs, urinary, and digestive tracts.

Mucous: Pertaining to or secreting mucus (free slime of the mucous membrane).

Neutrophils: White blood cells that stain neutral pink on hematoxylin and eosin (H&E) preparation.

Oxidation: A chemical reaction that takes place when a substance comes into contact with oxygen or another oxidising substance.

Pathology: Abnormality in the body.

Perennial: Existing for a long or apparently infinite time.

Photophobia: Burning sensation in eyes on exposure to light.

Pollens: Fine powdery substance discharged from flowers.

Pro-Inflammatory Mediators: Capable of causing inflammation.

Pruritus: Itchy skin.

Serum: The clear, watery portion of the blood after centrifuge.

Sinuses: Empty well-aerated box-like structures of different shapes and sizes in the skull.

Steatorrhoea: Steatorrhea (or steatorrhoea) is the presence of excess fat in faeces.

Symbiosis: A mutually beneficial relationship between different people or groups.

Systemic Allergic Reaction: An allergic reaction involving parts of the body distant from the actual site of allergen contact.

Subepithelial: Situated beneath an epithelial layer (layer covering all the body cavities and surface).

Turbinate: A curled shelf of bone that protrudes into the nasal cavity.

Treating Through: It is the continuation of a drug treatment in the presence of a developing or established drug hypersensitivity reaction.

Villi: Any of the finger-like projections from the intestine to help in the absorption of nutrients.

Abbreviations

AAP: American Academy of Pediatrics

AD: Atopic Dermatitis

ADHD: Attention-Deficit/Hyperactive Disorder

ASD: Autistic Spectrum Disorder

CDC: Centre for Disease Control

CMPA: Cow's Milk Protein Allergy

DBPCFC: Double-Blind Placebo-Controlled Food Challenge

FSSAI: Food Safety and Standards Authority of India

FA: Food Allergy

GI: Gastro Intestinal

HFSS: High in Fats, Salt, or Sugar

IAP: Indian Academy of Pediatrics

IM: Intramuscular

IV: Intravenous

JUNCS: Acronym to cover junk foods, ultra-processed foods, nutritionally inappropriate foods, caffeinated/coloured/carbonated foods/beverages, and sugar-sweetened beverages

LOE: Level of Evidence

NHS: National Health Services

SPT: Skin Prick Test

SSB: Sugar-Sweetened Beverages

USFDA: United States Food and Drug Administration

WHO: World Health Organization